Blood at Alamance!
The Murder Of Innocence:
A Governor's Guilt

Blood at Alamance!

The Murder Of Innocence: A Governor's Guilt

DR. JOSEPH BLAIR TURNER

ISBN: 978-0-578-18192-9
LIBRARY OF CONGRESS NO: 2016909787

NATHAN HOUSE BOOKS ®

BLOOD AT ALAMANCE!

© 2009 Joseph Blair Turner, Ph.D.

© 2015 Nathan House Books ®
P.O. Box 1696 ~ Oakwood, GA 30566 USA
NathanHouseBooks@yahoo.com

~ All Rights Reserved ~

No part of this book shall be reproduced, stored in a retrieval system, or transmitted by any means without written permission from the author.

Printing History:
1st Printing

PRINTED IN USA

Dedication

To my brother
Jarrett Stephen Turner,
stalwart, brave, and true:
Your memory is a lasting
Strength to all who knew you

To our fifth great-grandparents
Robert and Mary Messer
And family,
And all those steadfast ones
Who sacrificed so much
That we may enjoy our
God-given right to Freedom

Prologue

This story is based on true historic events which happened to real people. Their sufferings have wrought our blessings.

Let us never forget that our freedom was purchased with a great price, and tyranny stands ever eager to again raise its ugly head in defiance of same, once we lose diligence ~

~ J. B. Turner

BLOOD AT ALAMANCE!

CHAPTER ONE

LASHING leather ripped through the flesh of screaming men tied to fences. Women and children ran shrieking from their houses. Men were forced at gunpoint to awaiting ropes slung from tree limbs, and swiftly hanged. Mournful families walked the frontier roads of North Carolina, homeless and hopeless as their livestock were driven off by raging men, often their barns and homes going up in flames behind them.

Robert Messer tossed and perspired on his corn-husk mattress as he lay dreaming on these events, replaying in his mind the horrors being inflicted upon his neighbors across the colony by ruthless and greedy government officials. Nocturnal dream or daylight reality, the ominous hand of colonial rule gave little reason for rest.

Lying still for a moment as the scenes of terror abated, his dreaming mind drifted back several years to images of redcoated soldiers shooting and bayoneting red skinned men, who were battering the soldiers with their handmade weapons and returning fire with their scant few muskets.

Three screaming Cherokee warriors rushed a Redcoat, waving their tomahawks and knives. He thrust his bayonet deeply into the abdomen of the center man, causing his face to turn from rage to absolute shock, quivering from the sudden agony. As his eyes fluttered toward unconsciousness, his two fellow tribesmen reached the soldier as he tried to pull his bayonet from the Cherokee. He could not fend them off as they bashed in his head and plunged blades into his chest and back. They flung him down, where he fell upon the dying body of his foe.

Looking around for another human target, the two Cherokees were overwhelmed by four charging Redcoats who made quick work of dispatching them with their bayonets. They quickly reloaded their muskets, then rushed

TURNER

up a wooded hill to rejoin their British comrades in the ongoing fight. In the thickets, more Cherokees crept swiftly into position to attack the British from front and rear. Soon the battle was again pitting man against man, battling for reasons unknown to the young Robert, as they struggled on in bloody earnest.

Robert tossed anew, calling out in his sleep, "Hilfst du, Vater! Help them fight!"

His father, a German immigrant to the frontier of colonial North Carolina, cradled him in his dream, hiding in the bushes, whispering, "Robert, wir können gegen sie nicht kämpfen! Vee cannot take arms against our Cherokee neighbors, nor our King's soldiers! Vee must sh'stay sh'till to see how it verks out!"

So would pass the night, until shortly before dawn when his fitful sleep was interrupted by a present commotion.

Robert bolted upright, awakened by the desperate sounds approaching his cabin: shouts, thundering horse hooves, a musket shot. He sprang to the floor in his nightshirt as his wife Mary, now startled awake, sat up in the moonlight beaming through the window.

"What is it, Robert?" she cried softly, yet with undeniable strain. "Where're ye going?"

"They've got somebody. *Again.*" Robert grabbed his musket and flung open the cabin door, dashing out into the cool Carolina moonlight in his nightshirt.

"No, wait!" Mary called, louder. "What can ye do, against King's men?" But Robert was already disappearing into the silvery night of the misty woods as she watched fearfully from the doorway. She closed her tired eyes and muttered a silent prayer.

Robert Messer, tall and broad at the shoulders, marched masterfully and unafraid. His dark black hair, now untied, fell about the nape of his neck. Beams of moonlight seeped through the tree leaves at intervals, illuminating the tight and determined expression on his ruddy complexion. Usually fair enough to reflect his German ancestry, his face and arms tanned quickly from working in his fields. His ruddy appearance in spring and summer, along with his dark hair, caused many to wonder if he were part Cherokee, his

BLOOD AT ALAMANCE!

family having been closely associated with them from earliest pioneer times.

But Robert was a German-American by heritage, with the ingrained independence of both peoples, balanced with the American sense of justice and fair play. He strode forth as if the scales of justice hung from his hand, seeking to mollify any mistreatment that may now be taking place on his land.

As he approached a clearing, he stopped abruptly at the sound of an old man pleading for mercy, surrounded now by three ruffians astride their mounts. Their quarry was a poor colonial farmer, on foot and carrying a humble gunny sack of corn. Robert recognized him as his neighbor, Old Man Reedy. Also among them was John Butler, the Orange County sheriff, dismounting his horse with a pistol in one hand, and a document protruding from his vest pocket.

"There now, we have thee!" cried one assailant as he reined up, spinning his horse about. "Ye'll answer to the King's justice!" Robert recognized him now as one of the sheriff's dubious deputies.

"But what've I done?" cried Reedy, his creaking, antique voice floating on the night air in its quaint British accent.

"Thievery!" growled the sheriff.

"Nay! 'Tis me own goods. Me rightful property, a-takin' to share with me pitiful crippled brother! I had an early crop this year, and..."

"Quiet!" shouted the sheriff, piercing the cool night air. "Ye've taken from the Royal Stores, bound for tithes and taxes to the Governor-General. For this, ye'll hang! Or pay a fine, if ye've five pounds about ye!"

"Aye," joined the second deputy. "And 'is Excellency will appreciate the corn!" The other deputy uttered a mocking laugh.

"Bind him!" the sheriff barked. "And should the begger resist, brain him!"

The henchmen dismounted, their muskets aimed at the quaking farmer. He was approaching eighty four in age, and his tattered clothes did not appear much younger.

TURNER

"Just a bag o' roastin' ears," he mumbled. "Just picked 'em from me field by the light o' the moon, and was headin' out early, to-ward..."

"Quiet, I say!" shouted the first deputy, as he leaned forward, attempting to strike his head with the heavy barrel of his musket.

"Hold it, there!" cried Robert, running from his cover in the woods. Men and horses startled at his brash entrance onto the scene of brutality. He began to level his musket at the extorters, but then regarding their authority, thought better of it. "What goes on here?"

"And who might ye be?" the sheriff demanded, as their barrels turned on him. "Are ye about the sorry business of hindering the King's justice? Answer or die, I say!"

"No. I just—that is, I am the owner of this property. I heard a disturbance..."

"Then ye'd best be turning toward home. Sun's nearly up, and the lady of the house may well be inquiring as to ye own whereabouts!" The sheriff snarled in contempt, as his henchmen laughed in derision.

"Or better still, step lively, and see can ye catch *her* a-comin' in from all hours!" the second deputy jeered. Robert took one brisk, bold step toward the taunting man, then checked his advance, as again their muskets aligned with his head.

"P'raps we need come inspect *your* stores, to determine if ye be a-hoarding the Governor's due?" the first deputy snapped, as the others chanted, "Aye!" and "Yea!"

Robert pondered the deputies' accents, both of them obviously having come from England to exploit the colonials of the frontier counties of North Carolina, a growing trend. Robert replied with renewed boldness, "Or perhaps ye fellows can take a closer inspection right here, and see that poor, honest people may be..."

"Choose ye words with loyal caution, I warn'ee!" snapped the sheriff.

"My loyalty has never been in question, sir. But I know this man. He is honorable, he earns what he has, he..."

BLOOD AT ALAMANCE!

The sheriff ignored him while pulling the folded paper from his vest. He seized Reedy by the arm and said, "I've here a warrant to confiscate all ye chattel and goods, to the farthing, on the matter of..."

"Eh?" squealed Reedy. "Why, 'tis robbery! I..."

"...on the matter of a delinquent debt owed to his esteemed honor, Leftenant Colonel Edmund Fanning, in the sum of eight pounds, four shillings."

"But I've paid it! Six times over, in interest alone. Critters, corn, furs. Just gave him a fine calf last month!"

"Yet nary a recompense in hard currency. A gentleman the likes of *he* has no need for such trade! And ye've no receipt. Now, have ye?"

"He forced it on me! He obliged me to accept his loan, to pay the new assessment on me land, and it not worth twenty pounds! And sign papers I could not read—under threat of indenturing me to..."

The first deputy swung down his heavy musket barrel, striking Reedy's head.

"Oh! *Mercy in Heaven!*" Reedy cried. "To think I'd live so long, to come to this! Hit weren't this bad in England!"

With instant reflexive action, Robert's musket swung upward as he shouldered it masterfully, aligning its ominous muzzle with the torso of the scoundrel.

"Take on no more debt that ye can repay, I warn'ee!" Robert shouted at the bully. "Ye be naught but larsonists in livery!"

"Traitor!" the sheriff yelled at Robert.

"Don't *you* take on me worries, Cap'n Robert!" urged Reedy, now regaining his concentration.

"Eh? *Captain*, ye say? And what mean you, man?" the deputy asked.

"Captain of militia!" the sheriff suddenly acknowledged. He had been distracted for a moment, holding Reedy's shoulder with one hand, while attempting to read the warrant to him in the moonlight. His eyes darted in jittery patterns all over Robert's stern face. "I see ye now!" As moonlight illuminated Robert's features, the sheriff gave it closer inspection. "A white Indian, as one

5

might say. He's Captain Robert Messer, late of Craven County. Now farming here in Orange."

"Ahh—and well that is," the deputy said, his tone now more courteous, though strained. "And our respects to ye."

"What purpose have ye here? And how do humble county servants come to have such fine mounts?" Robert asked, as stern and brave as when he left his house.

The deputy leaned forward, and with a sneer, said, "We are about the Governor's errand. That sort of business is of no concern to the colonials."

"Ah, Cap'n Messer. German name, British subject, Cherokee defender," the sheriff remarked. "Ye look white, yet ye do favor the red. In just whose camp do ye stand?"

"I am a loyal subject of the King. My kin came to New Bern from the Pennsylvania Germans, true. And—as for the Cherokee—my father was in council with their mountain chiefs, and was called a chief by some."

"*Cherokee!* Had enough trouble with *them*. Army gave 'em the King's Justice, though!" the third deputy remarked.

"*And*—the Governor's *bayonets!*" added the second deputy. A flash of rage across Robert's face was easily detected by the rogue, who cooled his tone quickly.

"You must consider, the Cherokee have justice as well," said Robert, softly yet with strength.

"Eh? Do ye speak treason, Cap'n Messer?" the sheriff demanded.

"I do not speak for the Cherokee. I stand for the King. But the Cherokee have a way of avenging their own. That, neither you nor I can stop." The lawmen seemed suddenly stupified at the concept of sparking another Indian uprising, by offending this keystone Messer. He was a bridge between the worlds of white and red which they dared not to cross. The Crown had suffered many years of bloody Indian battles in North Carolina.

Slowly the sheriff gathered his thoughts, and his eyes seemed to again focus on Robert. "And ye say, ye be loyal to the Crown? Can that be substantiated in court? We may soon find out."

As if in orchestration, a body of men surged from every direction of the woods, some twenty in number, with their

BLOOD AT ALAMANCE!

muskets aimed at the sheriff and his rogue lawmen. They were Robert's neighbors, fellow militiamen from his own company.

"We heered musketry, Cap'n," announced one of the men. "Is all well, hereabout?"

Robert turned about, nodding at the man. He returned his attention to the sheriff, remarking, "Of no concern, ye say? It would appear *you* have *new* concerns at the moment. But here, take a message to your Colonel Fanning. Tell him we are petitioning the Governor for due rights as Royal subjects. Advise him that we who stand for King and colony, will not stand for tyranny in the guise of authority. Mind ye well our numbers, and intentions. Now, ride out!"

As Robert's men stood their ground and gripped their muskets tightly in the face of tyranny, seeds of independence were being planted and the American Spirit being postured, though they could not have recognized it at the time.

One by one the intruders turned their steeds toward the road, then stopped and looked back at the sheriff. He waved his document in the direction of Robert and his elderly friend, penetrating the early air with an uneasy admonition. "Just mind ye well, Messer. The accounts will soon be balanced. I answer to Superior Court, and to the well-seated Assemblyman, Fanning. And he, to Governor-General Tryon!"

Robert stood rooted like a statue as the sheriff remounted. Man and beast turned slowly away into the coming dawn. The poor farmer, Reedy, was left with a bag of corn, a mind of confusion, and a heart of gratitude. The outlaw lawmen didn't even demand the expected "nuisance fee" extortion, usually consisting of whatever was in a person's pocket.

"Two-legged weasels, they be!" Reedy quietly observed. "Where do they grow such critters? Noah never boarded 'em."

"Get on home, old friend. The hungry hounds'll not have blood this day," Robert consoled the farmer. "Nor corn." Reedy shook Robert's left hand, his right hand still

TURNER

rubbing the knot atop his head. Reedy, the aged colonial, stood with feet in two worlds: One in the crumbling old, and another in the hopeful new whose birthing pains were only too soon about to commence.

"Hark'ee!" the old farmer whispered. "Another's a-comin', through the woods yonder!"

Robert wheeled about with his musket, then relaxed to see it was Mary. His confident smile was visible through the rising dawn, evoking a feebler yet sweetly sincere smile of her own. The men folk, embarrassed that Mary was still in her nightgown, turned to leave as swiftly as they had arrived, vanishing into the shadowy woods. Reedy turned his eyes away modestly, as he retrieved his sack of corn.

"Thank'ee kindly, Robert. I'll be on me way," the farmer said as he walked onward. He kept nodding and saying, "Thank'ee, Thank'ee," embarrassed to look back.

Mary, now discomfited to see other men present, modestly darted behind a wide oak tree. Robert crept silently to the near side, then leaning his musket against it, reached around and took Mary suddenly in his arms. He silenced her startled voice with a soothing kiss, warming the cool morning air about them. He could sense her uneasiness as she trembled in his arms, but continued to hold her and assure her that all was well—for the moment.

Mary was the essence of pure womanhood: her small and rounded shoulders adorned with flowing brown hair that glistened in any degree of light—her tender yet confident face so lovely it was born to be admired and caressed—her lithe figure flowing poetically as she walked, yet with a self-assured poise that commanded respect. Above all, her soft, sweet voice was matched only by her pure and loving spirit, a living branch from the vine of bliss. Her standards of righteousness were balanced perfectly by her benchmark paradigm of fairness. She could have been equally at home in a palace or a pioneer cabin, her graciousness gaining the instant respect of all who encountered her.

Robert silently counted his blessings as he held and caressed this rare treasure he thankfully called *wife*, as she soothed the savagery of the night from his mind and soul.

BLOOD AT ALAMANCE!

Back in the cabin, the children were rousting from their beds in the open loft. Ten year old Christian climbed down the ladder, rubbed his eyes, and looked up with smiling admiration at his fine father. After their hug, Christian eyed the musket and the dew on Robert's bare feet, and asked in his polite tone, "What, Paw? Are ye a-huntin' so early?"

"And in your nightshirt?" added eleven year old Tipton, with a giggle.

"Thought I heard a nuisance, 'tis all," replied their stoic father.

"Tipton, Christian, Solomon!" Mary began to call. "Joseph, Jarred, Mary-Ann! Up and about." A row of young faces now peered over the edge of the loft floor. "Prayers. Get clothed. Wash up. Day's a-breakin'!" A rooster began to crow, confirming her observation.

Mary fried salt-cured ham and corn fritters on the open fire as Robert dressed in his finer clothes.

"A-going to meetin' again?" Mary asked.

"Well, yes. Herman Husband's a-coming to speak. His ideas are best, for regulating the corruption we endure."

"Oh, Robert!" Mary cried out, laying aside her cabin culinaries. "I'm a-feared this path will only lead to bloodshed! Or charges of treason!"

"We only want to appeal to the Governor for regulation. We mean no treachery." He pulled a folded paper from his inner breast pocket and handed it to her. "See, hit's Herman's latest pamphlet. His ideas for reform are peaceable. Besides, he's a Quaker. He'll do naught that would lead to a fight."

"But simply to assemble; to complain. Do ye not fear the consequences?"

"We *have* an Assembly to represent us, in New Bern. Yet they lack the courage to make a change. Herman introduced proposals to end corruption, then somehow the Governor held sway over the majority of Assemblymen, to quiet him. Some of them profit from our abuse. We should have rallied and planned our appeal more effectively, while Herman still sat in the Assembly!" Despite limited educational opportunities, Robert and Mary possessed a native intelligence which facilitated their ability to converse astutely on topics of social importance. Their dignified bearing gave them a prominence among the common folk, whom they loved and served with graceful humility.

"But Herman was arrested I hear, for speaking in Assembly against corrupt taxes!"

"That be true. But he was freed by a mob of armed farmers who marched on the jail."

"And now you, Robert—you want to march into Herman's camp and..." Mary's head dropped as tears gushed, muffling her words, "...and reserve your own place on the gallows!"

Robert lifted her head gently by the chin, and wiped her wet cheeks. "We have to make a movement now, while the spirit moves amongst us. Hit's act, or die."

"But, by what means? What influence can mere colonials have, against such powers?"

"Hit's nothing so drastic as the marches on New Bern, nor the Sons of Liberty refusing to allow the Stamp Act in the colony. Surely Tryon will see the Regulation Movement as a better way out of his quandary. Why, most of upper Carolina stands against him, and when he comes to see that..."

Mary looked sadly toward the cabin floor. The hand-hewn boards were a rugged contrast to her silken beauty and soft manner. Yet the rough surface was a comparative luxury, their cabin being one of the few in Orange County without an earthen floor.

Robert sat down on a handcrafted wooden chair, and pulled Mary down onto his lap. With his arm around her, she went on. "I know, hit's all true. Every time a new county is formed, the new sheriff, and courts, and registry men—and tax men—even the clarks—begin to impose fees for this, fees for that..."

"And they are always heavily imposed, with malice. The Eastern dandies draw their share, and laugh at the frontier farmers as though they were born to be ill-treated, and extorted to their last shilling!" Robert calmed himself on realizing he was drawing the attention of the children. "And now the county militias are taking sides for and

BLOOD AT ALAMANCE!

against Tryon. What will it mean? How will it end? We want the King's justice, is all."

"Well, I hope ye'll get it from the King's puppet, Bully Billy!" Mary smiled through her anxiety. It was enough to thaw Robert's frozen face, as smile met smile for another reassuring kiss.

Little Mary-Ann looked up from her breakfast, grinning. "Bully Billy's crooked as a barrel full of fish hooks," she said. Her commentary was both innocent and shrewd. Mary jumped up from Robert's lap and returned to her cooking.

"Now, my sweet little traitor! Be that treason that ye speak?" Robert adored her innocence, yet inwardly trembled to think of where her honesty could lead. Truth and liberty often did not coexist in the colony.

"Her heart speaks true. Let your words today do into the bargain. But don't ye speak us clear to the gallows!" her mother interjected. Then turning to her daughter, she added, "And you, wee one, mind out what ye say! The woods have ears that reach plumb to New Bern!"

Robert and Mary let their eyes sink into one another's gaze, sharing an expression that was meant to be reassuring, yet sparked with uncertainty. So deep was their sense of justice, yet so much larger seemed the unjust. Like youthful waders suddenly swept into a swift current, they could no more resist the pull of duty than they could the overpowering stream of evil now engulfing their very existence.

A parting kiss in the open doorway added to the gentle warmth now coming from the rising sun. After hugs and kisses to daughter and sons all 'round, Robert doffed his tri-corner hat and took the reins of his horse Atticus from Tipton, and mounted. Christian handed him his musket. "See to the critters, and mind Mother," he admonished with a smile. He veered his steed down the road toward the meeting ground. He turned and waved his hat to his admiring boys, who stood waving until he was out of sight.

The sun filtered through the lush canopy of hardwood trees along the road, stirring the heart to rapture at nature's beauty. Yet within the natural serenity lurked the antithesis of harmony. Unseen by Robert were two sets of

TURNER

eyes peering at him through the woods, eyes belonging to men who served as extensions of the eyes of Edmund Fanning. Taking note of his departure, they hastily turned their horses to ride away as if on an errand of urgency.

Yet Robert rode happily on, contented for the moment in the arboreal ambiance that blended with his own positive outlook concerning the task that lay before him.

Occasionally there would be a break in the dense frontier forest, to reveal a struggling yet well kept farm carved out by honest, ever-laboring hands. He could not help drifting into a reverie of bitter times and harsh events that had interposed themselves, accentuating highlights within this idyllic painting. Colonial farmers and their beasts moved about upon nature's canvas, farms and families bloomed, yet colonial tyrants lurked about the thorny edges and in the dark of the woods. Bounty beckoned to the motivated and independent worker, but progress was checked and deformed by sanctioned parasites. Paradise was infected.

CHAPTER TWO

THE long ride ahead gave Robert time to reflect. His mind drifted back through the conflicts of the last five years, his nerve hardening at the tyranny of the corrupt government—the false taxes followed by false criminal charges—as fee was added upon fee. Decent but desperate people were threatened into accepting small loans or goods from sheriffs, tax officials or chief magistrates, then arrested when they could not repay the debts and exorbitant interest. Then their families would be turned out of their homes, while their crops and livestock were illegally confiscated by the very sheriffs who should have protected them. Every appeal to the courts and governor had either been ignored, or met with more legal threats, even charges of treason leading to banishment or execution.

Robert ruminated over the accounts of one of Sheriff Butler's many recent travesties. Butler had cast an eye of envy toward Thaddeus Ledford's fine new stallion as he rode through Hillsborough. Thaddeus was a man of common roots, but who carried himself with uncommon dignity, dressed neatly, and exuded a self-confident respectability. Wise management of his farming interests had led to a small but profitable mercantile suppliership which afforded him the means to obtain such a fine mount. He sat tall in the saddle, entering town with such subtle yet tasteful flair that man and steed moved practically as one entity.

Butler observed him with piercing eyes, seeming to project a deep resentment of his success and good fortune. Scrutinizing Thaddeus as he rode into the center of town, he growled out to his two deputies, "Broley! Jep! Arrest him!"

TURNER

The two men stepped in front of him and leveled pistols at his torso, as one of them cried out, "Get down. Ye're under arrest!"

"What? Me? What do you..."

The men pulled him off his saddle while Butler took hold of the horse's reins.

"On the charge of nonpayment of taxes," Butler barked, grimacing fiercely.

"Just wait'll I get you'uns in court," Thaddeus sputtered, pulling against the grips that the men held on his arms.

"Court?" retorted Broley with a broad grin. Both deputies laughed aloud.

"No need for court, Ledford," Butler dictated. "We got ye dead to rights!"

"Ye'll have to prove *that*," Thaddeus snapped sternly, as the men tied his hands behind his back. He was pushed and pulled into the jail, but on entering gave no more resistance.

Butler took pen and paper and handed to Jep, saying in a quiet tone seemingly laced with embarrassment, "Uh, write this down for me, will ye?" His illiteracy and lack of breeding were a hinderance to his prospects to climb socially, though he was forever contriving means to obtain personal financial advancement. He turned to Thaddeus and resumed his louder tone of voice. "Now, Ledford, ye're under suspicion of nonpayment of taxes..."

"I owe nary a thing! Honestly, now, ye know that, don't ye?"

"...and add to that obstruction of justice, arrest expense, and general nuisance fees. The fine will be five shillings on each charge. Search him!"

Now Thaddeus began to fend them off as well as he could, with his loose legs. They scuffled around in a circle like mad fighting roosters. He was grabbed about the chest by Jep, as Broley struck his head with his fist, knocking his new tri-corner hat to the floor where it got crushed by thrashing feet. After Broley took him in a choke hold and smashed his face into the wall a couple of times, he slumped down to the floor.

BLOOD AT ALAMANCE!

"Naught but a shilling and sixpence in his pockets, Sheriff," Jep reported.

"Then hit's thirty days in jail. And forfeiture of the horse, pending proof of a bill of sale showing ownership. The proof is required to be shown within seven days."

Thaddeus pled through bleeding lips, "Let me send a message to my folks."

The lawless lawmen laughed as he was untied and pushed into a poorly lit cell, devoid of furnishings other than a tattered old blanket. Slumped against the wall, he could do little more than stare in shock and disbelief for the better part of an hour. He closed his eyes and passed the rest of the day in prayer and meditation. Just before sundown a woman came in with a basket and handed it to Jep. He and Broley sat it on a table within his view, and withdrew baked potatoes, boiled corn, and raw turnips, which they promptly sat and devoured.

"Hit's lucky to have an early corn crop this year, even if hit's just these little nubbin' ears," Jep opined through glutinous chomping.

"Druther have an early crop of shillings and pounds!" Laughed Broley, wiping his mouth with his sleeve.

Seeing Thaddeus' pining eyes, Broley carried a turnip over to the bars and called out, "Hyar, Ledford, ketch this." Then he paused, withdrew a knife, and cut the turnip in half. "Naw, better save half fer breakfast!" He tossed the turnip half in to Thaddeus, which he pounced upon with gusto. Suddenly he paused, reflected, and closed his eyes to utter a humble prayer of thanks. Broley returned to the table where Jep cast a broad smirk at the site, and consumed the remaining piece of turnip.

Shortly after daybreak, Jep tossed half a raw potato into the cell. "Too bad about ye horse," he taunted.

Thaddeus looked at him with piercing, curious eyes, while hungrily gobbling down the potato portion. He scratched all over from the new visitors in his clothing: bedbugs which thrived within the old blanket.

"Hit's a purdee sight, ain't it, Broley, to see an upstart having to scrounge fer a bite to eat, like us common folks!"

TURNER

Still chomping the last bits of this meager repast, he managed to mutter, "What d'ye mean, my horse?"

Jep laughed derisively, "Why, hit was forfeited! What'd ye think?"

Thaddeus grabbed the bars and now retorted, "How? Why?"

"Nonpayment of fines and fees." Jep shook his head and smirked as he turned away.

"And taxes, of some sort or'nuther," Broley chimed in with a mocking grin.

"So, what's next? Gonna kill me off? For ye know this will be tolt once I get outta here!"

Since he was not allowed to send messages to anyone to come relieve his situation, the horse was forfeited and sold to the sheriff's cousin in neighboring Guilford County for one fourth its value.

After four days of living on halves of turnips and potatoes, Jep threw open the cell and gruffly proclaimed, "Out with ye! We're tired o'feedin' ye!"

"Besides, ye aint got nuthin' left of any interest to us!" Broley chimed in. "And nobody's comin' a-lookin' fer ye. So git on outta hyar!"

Thaddeus sat peering in wonder. He hesitated in standing; partly from hunger draining his energies, as well as the mere shock of the unexpected discharge.

Jep kicked at his boot and snarled, "Yew heered 'im! Git ye hide on outta hyar!"

With much effort Thaddeus put on his disfigured hat, came to his feet, and stumbled toward the door and onto the dirt street, shielding his weak eyes from the unexpected beams of sunlight. Weak from near-starvation, he dragged his feet along the street. The faint feeling of freedom began to stream into his troubled mind just as Butler stepped around a corner of the building and quipped sarcastically, "Ye don't look so fine n' dandy now, do ye, Ledford? And ye thought ye was a high-stepping gentleman! Ha ha ha!"

"We will have our day of reckoning, Butler," came Thaddeus' humble but solid reply.

BLOOD AT ALAMANCE!

"Well, look'ee here! Ain't learned his lesson." Butler looked toward the deputies with a sneer. Turning back to Thaddeus, he grumbled, "Looks like I'll have to arrest ye for public staggering!"

"What're ye gonna fine me now, Butler?" came Thaddeus' strained reply. "What've I got left, that you want?"

Butler rocked back and forth on his feet, his eyes darting about in a puzzled flutter. He started to turn away with a gesture of dismissal by his hand, then paused and turned back. Looking at Thaddeus' new boots, then down at his own feet, he discerned they wore the same size. Then he growled, "Ye don't need them big fancy boots. They'll just make ye stagger and get into more trouble. Jep—Broley—relieve him of them burdensome boots."

The men forced him to sit on the dirt street as they tugged at his boots. He was too weak to resist. With a glinting jingle, coins fell from inside one boot, onto the dirt.

"Three shillings!" cried Broley. They frantically shook and reached into both boots, searching for more treasure.

"That be his fine! Now, remove his sorry carcass from my sight. Deposit him on the county line!" Broley handed the shillings and boots to Butler, who held them in opposite hands, looking at silver and then leather, as if weighing out their respective values. Apparently sensing the boots were not easily marketable, he handed one shilling apiece to both deputies and pocketed the other. He looked the boots over once more, and tossed them at Thaddeus.

Thaddeus grabbed for his boots as they pulled him to his feet. Broley brought up a wagon and they tossed him in the back. Once they reached the county line, Jep made a gesture with a jerk of his thumb, signaling for him to exit the wagon. Slowly striving to crawl out the back, impeded by exhaustion and aches, Broley popped the reins and made the horse start, tossing Thaddeus onto the ground. Broley turned the vehicle around and they rode off unceremoniously, without so much as looking back.

Two hours later his brother Jamison, returning by wagon from Guilford County, saw the figure of a man sprawled out on the roadside. He reined up, slowing the wagon, and rode cautiously over toward the man as he came into nearer view. Seeing no present danger, he called out, "Hello there. You, sir. Are you alright?" No answer was forthcoming. "I say there. May I be of assistance?"

The motionless body now began to move slightly as Thaddeus tried to raise himself up on his elbows. "Wait, let me help you," Jamison declared. Thaddeus recognized Jamison's voice and turned onto his side, attempting a feeble smile.

Jamison began to kneel down to assist him, then jerked back in shock before exclaiming, "Oh, good Heavens! Thaddeus! It's you!"

"Me as ever was me," Thaddeus answered with a groan.

"But—but—whatever happened to you?"

"Butler happened to me! Sheriff Butler and his rogues."

Jamison took him to the McGinnis Inn, nearby. After resting for a few reflective moments, he untied the mare he was leading from the back of the wagon, and wrote Thaddeus a permit to ride the horse home. "Now you take the long way 'round, and avoid Hillsborough. Ye hear?" Jamison admonished.

It was the next day before Thaddeus felt sufficiently rested and nourished to head home. Nevertheless too tired for a long ride, he defiantly rode back through Hillsborough. In the center of town a wiry and weathered figure leaned backward on a hitching rail, mopping his wet brow with a handkerchief, obscuring his face. His brown hair hung to the shoulders. Thaddeus squinted to recognize him. As the man returned his bandana to his pocket and tied his hair back at the nape of his neck, his visage became instantly familiar: Sheriff Butler!

Both men looked stunned as eye met eye. Butler ran up and seized his reins, fumed, and spurted, "About time ye came to pay ye back taxes! Still got no money about ye, now, I wager!" Then lowly he groaned aloud, "Jep and Broley, you'uns had to be gone when I needed ye, didn't ye!" Then louder again, he said with rage, "I'll be a-taking the horse for taxes owed!"

BLOOD AT ALAMANCE!

As Thaddeus attempted to turn the horse about, Butler pulled his pistol and ordered him off. Then suddenly three passersby ran up in a rage, retrieved the reins from Butler, and returned them to Thaddeus. The victim and his trio of rescuers stood staring at the equally astonished sheriff. They mounted and rode away before the sheriff could begin to shout, "Arrest them! Traitors! This be treason!" But his voice met no willing ears.

Butler had difficulty assembling a posse to pursue them, crying out, "You men there! Mount up and ride with me! Mount up, I say, while I fetch my horse!" But no one responded. The few townspeople starred at him blankly. "Rabble! Treasonous trash!" he grumbled at those who declined to join him, mentally marking down their names for future retribution. He failed to appreciate the deeper current of resistance among the colonists, which indeed was spreading throughout the frontier counties of North Carolina.

Thaddeus fled at full gallop into Guilford County. Two days later he spied his stolen horse as it was being ridden by Butler's brother. Watching and waiting while the man dismounted and hitched the horse to a post at Guilford Court House, he rode over and cautiously untethered his stallion's reins, and "stole" him back, leading him up the road and into the countryside.

As Robert Messer drifted through these daydreams, a low limb brought his attention back to the road before him. He hummed awhile, nibbled on a ham biscuit Mary had given him, and soon his thoughts were adrift again. Reminiscences of his father supplying flour, hams, and other foodstuffs to the Cherokee for trade goods soon hooked his thoughts onto those childhood years filled with awe and adventure—yet punctuated with acute tragedies. He would ameliorate the horror and sadness of the British and Cherokee wars, with proud reflections of the days when his father helped broker peace between the two warring factions.

These and many troubling memories streamed through Robert's mind in a continuous flow. Only occasionally would the awareness come to mind that he was drowning

TURNER

in musings of misery, whereupon he would shake his head and attempt to focus on something else.

He began to reflect instead upon the solid goodness of his family. How very good they were. And how good a life they could lead, and how very much they could contribute to Carolina, if—only if. Many ifs now began to surface, pricking into consciousness his worries for the future of his worthy family, and the many potential pitfalls the unregulated tyrant Tryon might place before them.

A duet of mockingbirds eased these dark reveries from Robert's mind, rendering a momentary respite from the reality at hand as he rode along the rural road through the idyllic landscape. A momentary pleasantness now nested in his mind as he reveled in nature's avian concert, breathed her fragrant air, and visually feasted upon her lovely verdant scenes. Yet just as fleeting as his memories of legal atrocities in Orange County were these welcomed musings, scurrying from his consciousness as again his mind returned to the task that lay before him.

CHAPTER THREE

 Butler called upon Lt. Col. Fanning at his residence. Reaching up to knock, he hesitated as he observed Fanning through the doorside window. Standing before a parlor mirror, Fanning was about the business of visually inspecting himself in his new uniform. Tall and lean with wavy dark-blond hair, he struck a good enough figure, though bearing a somewhat babyish face. He practiced standing erect and stern, tightening his face to effect a formidable and commanding look.
 He strapped on his sword and, with hand on handle, jiggled the sword once while jerking his head in a snappy fashion. He would turn to the left, then to the right, all the time keeping his vain eyes trained upon his image. He rubbed his hair back on both sides, smoothed his eyebrows, and again snapped to an erect statuesque position.
 Seeming satisfied with these aspects, he went on to inspect his long narrow nose by running his finger along it, then flicked his round cheek with the end of his thumb as if to make it grow inward. His long narrow ears suited the nose, and overall his pudgy face presented a good balance of features except for the shallowness of the chin, which accentuated the roundness of the juvenile face. One more leering, snobbish expression in the mirror, followed by one of sternness, then he set about admiring his striking new apparel.
 Fanning was attired in a dashing red and gold uniform so finely made, it rivaled anything the money-grabbing Governor Tryon could boast. In fact, Fanning patronized Tryon's own tailor in New Bern, providing explicitly detailed instructions and professionally sketched diagrams to clearly show just how he wanted his uniform to appear. So much gold trim was artfully applied, that it distracted from the red

fabric of the coat. His sole focus in life seemed to be attaining the status and appearance—and ultimately the power—enjoyed by Tryon.

Yet Fanning was no upstart; he was the only graduate of Yale University residing in the entire colony. His family roots were impressive enough. Through their political connections he was able to secure a position of enviable power in the colony on the Governor's Council, ostensibly to serve a land and a people for whom he cared nary a whit. His only love was for power and riches. He was absorbing the riches fast enough, but so craved greater power that he continually vaunted himself to at least appear to walk among the political giants of his time.

After all, he had successfully ingratiated himself to Governor Tryon by flattery—spiced with contributions of funds raised through exorbitant taxation. And Tryon, despite his bearish manner, was no political slouch, himself having been directly appointed Royal Governor of North Carolina by King George III. But Fanning wanted to rise to higher powers than Assemblyman or Colonel of Militia. His recent years as Crown Attorney, clerk of superior court, and briefly as a probate judge, were only stepping stones to the political arena. He had his dreams set upon a governorship in New York or Massachusetts, followed by a return to England as a man of means; perhaps even knighthood or a seat in Parliament.

So out in the provincial gleaning grounds Fanciful Fanning garnered his lucre, amassing a fortune toward his hopeful day of influence and supremacy. Indeed, he already cut quite an aristocratic figure strolling about his plantation near Hillsborough, as if continually rehearsing his next visit to the Governor's mansion in New Bern. He expended far more time in social boasting and name-dropping than he did mingling among the effete and powerful social circles of the colony.

His slaves and passersby often observed him with amusement, as he walked about the plantation practicing elitist salutations and flattering language to use in New Bern. "*Bonjour, Monsieur de Gouveneur,*" or "*Tres*

BLOOD AT ALAMANCE!

enchanteé, Madame Tryon!" he would rehearse, with a feigned French intonation.

Yet the first time Fanning tried out his French niceties on Tryon, the governor's face turned red as he snapped, "I'll thank you to forego the use of French in my presence, Colonel, and to remember I received two wounds here (pointing to his thigh) and two here (pointing to his head), at the hands of the French at Cherbourg!" Ever determined to climb the social ladder, the undaunted Fanning would simply go on to find other ways to curry favor with his superiors.

Though over thirty, he had never married. "Too in love with himself," scoffers would say, "to waste himself on a bride!" Yet when the notion struck his fancy, he would take up serious company with attractive women who were unfortunate enough to cross his field of vision. He would hound them mercilessly, coercing them into accepting his company at public gatherings where he could show himself off by parading his unwilling ladies. And ladies he viewed as just another form of riches to be exploited. Heaven help the innocent woman who was ever manipulated into his private company, alone and defenseless with this heartless, self-worshipping beast.

Sensing Fanning's self-adoration ritual would go on forever, Butler finally rapped on the door. Fanning spun around and swiftly removed his sword, placing it in a corner while his servant answered the door.

"Sheriff Butler to see the Colonel," he said tersely, lacking Fanning's attempt at elitism or verbal flourish, though equally power-hungry. On seeing the lovely woman who answered the door, Butler looked up at the brim of his hat, and embarrassedly removed it with a nod of courtesy.

"Directly, sir," the woman meekly replied. She was a refined and breathtaking beauty, not the kind to be expected to be in service. He thought her a woman of social standing rather than a mere domestic. He stood admiring her with awe, trailing her every movement with his eyes as she turned to call out to Fanning, "Colonel, Sheriff Butler…"

TURNER

"Ah, yes, do come in, Butler," Fanning called from within.

"Shall I serve refreshment, Colonel?" the servile angel meekly inquired of Fanning.

With a brief but fixed look at the maid, intense with apparent but restrained infatuation, he replied, "That will be all, Cordelia."

Butler stepped into the vestibule as Fanning handed his empty glass to the maid, without offering any to Butler. Fanning motioned him toward the parlor and, attempting to hide his look of disgust at the sight of this rumpled commoner in his presence, manually bade him take a seat. Though their individual stations in life were ranked vastly apart, their grungy hearts belonged in the same sty; though Fanning, if indeed a hog within a sty, would naturally endeavor to stand atop the backs of the other swine.

"Some of the Governor's own troops are patrolling the area," the sheriff began. "We could dispatch word to Governor Tryon by them, to hasten some reliable forces to quell these upstart rebels..."

"And surrender control?" snapped Fanning, leaning forward across the table, exchanging his lofty and detached pose for one of alert control. "Billy—er, that is, the Governor—needn't worry himself with our local affairs. Should he feel the need to come take control of our little domain, you will feel it erode from beneath your feet. Yet if we secure the colonials ourselves, shooing them from beneath his worried wig, how much more shall he be impressed! Even to the point of, shall we say, *reward?*

"Shall we start with the court, then?" Butler squinted his eyes as if focusing on something intangible—or some budding concept—just beginning to come into view. Apparently now he began to see the benefit of playing the legal system, as opposed to singular acts of violence as a means of gaining wealth and power.

"Right thinking, my man! Fill the docket with those accused of—well, whatever they need accusing of!"

Butler looked away toward the window as if in deep contemplation. After all, if this thug wanted what Fanning

BLOOD AT ALAMANCE!

had, he should play by Fanning's system and methodology. There was much to consider and learn.

Fanning cast his eyes for another singular, searing moment at the sight of Cordelia Ownbey, the young spring flower of a woman ensnared amongst his unhappy domestic staff. His gaze pierced through her, filling her with anxiety as if, within that sheer moment, she detected the potential for longer and more overbearing encounters with him.

Cordelia was the picture of innocent loveliness. Her face combined tender beauty with deep purity, in a balance that won immediate admiration and respect from all who looked upon her; and the gaze of admirers would linger as long as propriety would allow. Her long blonde hair shone like spun gold. Fanning had ordered her to wear it down, rather than up as most women did during daylight hours, adding embarrassment to her already meek nature. Petite but well formed, she walked like a gentle breeze and seemed to trail the fragrance of spring flowers in her wake.

She was from a family of more than moderate means and refinement, though possessing that intrinsic elegance that comes from heart and spirit, an inner trait enviable by those of nobler birth and rank. Gracious and a seeker of grace, she had nonetheless become an impoverished lass. She needed Fanning's employment and shelter, as she and James Few jointly saved toward their intended day of marriage. She darted past the parlor and out of Fanning's view, while he lingered momentarily within selfish thoughts of her, contemplating how to erase this beloved James Few from her life.

How courtly he had behaved upon first meeting her during probate court in Hillsborough, graciously offering to take her into his employ when her parents died. As the judge settled their estate, declaring their home must be seized to pay dubious taxes, Fanning exploited the opportunity to smoothly explain the advantage of domestic servitude, which would provide lodging for her within his mansion.

TURNER

The judge had given a knowing look at Fanning as he revealed to the under-aged Cordelia her father had been delinquent in his taxes.

"Oh, no," she had protested, her meekness and manners being the only cap upon her sudden seizure of anxiety. "Papa was always so fastidious—exacting in his accounts and obligations..."

Cordelia had finally lost her self-composure to the point that she began to weep, quietly and softly, fighting back the emergence of a heavy sob.

Fanning had reached over and patted her hand, patronizing in his feigned words of comfort: "There, now, Miss Ownbey. There, now." Fanning and the judge again made furtive glances at each other, both expressing anxiety over how to end this uncomfortable scene.

"I knew your honorable father, Miss Ownbey," Fanning went on. "That is why I appeared at this hearing, to lend comfort to the daughter of a worthy friend whom I held in the highest esteem." She had then laid her head on his shoulder and let the precious tears roll as he went on. "And hence my requesting of the court to grant me custody of you, Miss Ownbey—Miss *Cordelia*, if I may—to provide you with shelter and security—indeed, employment—until you come of age."

When the judge made a motion with his head for Fanning to remove her from the courtroom, he gladly obliged, taking her by her tender arm and assisting her from her chair and out to his waiting carriage.

Once he had gotten her home, Fanning had virtually imprisoned her. Keeping her under his constant watch, he never allowed her to leave the house unescorted, or to receive guests unchaperoned by him. He exerted such possessive and interruptive tension in social settings that her acquaintances eventually came less and less often, until she was practically friendless. Fanning never let up in dominating her life; and adding an element of jeopardy which tormented her ceaselessly, he waited with the scrutiny of a vulture for the opportunity to make her his next amorous trinket.

BLOOD AT ALAMANCE!

James Few had somehow always managed to be in town whenever Cordelia was allowed one of her rare trips from the plantation, and attempted to speak with her until Fanning or another escort would make excuses to move on, leaving James to stare at her sad departure.

Once James had summoned the courage to call on her at home, she would only talk to him through the door, explaining woefully that she was not allowed to receive guests without Fanning present. It was when Fanning had learned of these brief visits upon his own domain that he had begun to concoct a way to foil their plans for marriage.

First Fanning had James' taxes exorbitantly over-appraised, within a scheme to continually add late fees and spurious penalties. He then manipulated James into his service to pay off the exorbitant interest on the loan he coerced him to accept, in order to pay the overcharge on his taxes. James was thus unable to properly attend to his own little farm, and was nearing an emotional crisis as he fell farther behind in his imposed obligations. And the farther he fell, the longer he and Cordelia had to postpone their marriage, all part of Fanning's manipulative scheming.

Today Cordelia watched longingly out a window to see James putting hay in the barn loft, alongside some field slaves. She would ameliorate at least some of her stress by humming a hymn while attending to her domestic duties. Hearing her in the adjoining room, Fanning became distracted and concluded his meeting with the sheriff. Rising from his seat, he walked him toward the foyer with the remark, "Now, see about your duties. Accounts balanced on behalf of King and colony, and all that."

"Aye, sir," replied the sheriff, nodding in obeisance as he donned his tri-cornered hat.

"One moment. As for that incident with the Ledford fellow…"

"Traitorous scroundrel, ye mean—sir."

"Why is he not yet in jail, awaiting trial?"

"Word is, sir, he's fled the county for good."

"Then who shall serve as his example-by-proxy?"

"Sir?"

TURNER

"His whipping-boy? Who shall be made an example for all, in his place? We must balance the books in all cases."

"Oh, I see. I'll be about it, sir. A lesson will indeed be learned—by all of the county!" The sheriff smiled wryly as he left the doorway. He turned back to offer Fanning his hand. Fanning was reluctant to accept it initially, but then gave him a limp handshake, followed by wiping his hand on the side of his tunic.

"And all of Carolina. For King and colony!" Then with a grimace Fanning added, "But within legal means. We must adhere to the—um—*proprieties*—at all times!"

"Right again, sir," came the sheriff's words as he walked across the yard toward his horse. He mounted and rode away, with his deputies close behind. He seldom left either of them behind to tend the office or watch the town, fearing more for his personal security due to the hatred he was cultivating throughout Orange County.

Fanning immediately swirled about and headed through the house in search of the lovely Cordelia, no longer able to resist her charms. Finding her at last as she dusted in the back parlor, he stood towering over her a moment, then broke the silence with "*Ahem*."

"I swan!" cried Cordelia, her skirts rustling as she spun around from the sudden alarm. Then on seeing her employer, she held her hand to her throat as she tried not to pant. "Oh, hit's you, sir. You gave me a start!"

Fanning continued standing and staring. Cordelia stood a moment, then turned to the side. Fanning took her by the arm and pulled her to himself as she strained to utter, "If ye'll excuse me, sir, I'll be going about..."

But her words turned to a muffled groan as Fanning pressed his lips to hers and held her tightly. She broke loose and tore open the back door, stumbling onto the porch. Fanning was in close pursuit. Without a word, he seized her again on the porch and attempted to force his oppressive presence upon her.

Out at the barn her suitor, James, was pitching hay down to the cattle.

With the instincts of both gentleman and lover, James jumped from the loft and bounded over the rail fence,

BLOOD AT ALAMANCE!

then sprinted like a deer toward the back porch. As he flew up the steps, Fanning drew a small pistol from beneath his coat and leveled it at James, whose body swayed to a stop as his feet riveted themselves to the porch planks.

"Stop! Or I'll blast you where you stand!" shouted Fanning.

Cordelia shrieked and fainted. James leapt nimbly forward and caught her in his arms. He held her gently, yet firmly, as a long-cherished treasure about to slip from sailor to sea. Looking into her pale face he called to her, "Cordie! Cordie! Speak to me!"

The shriek brought three field slaves and the two enslaved house workers running toward the porch, then halting in their tracks upon seeing Fanning trembling with his pistol, still pointing it toward James. He was still trembling when the sheriff and deputies rode swiftly to the back yard, reining up at the porch. The three men brandished pistols and leveled them at James.

James ignored the impending threat and called to one of the field hands, "Hector, fetch her a gourd of cool water!" Hector started toward the well, but then checked his action as he looked to his master Fanning for approval. Fanning nodded lightly, and Hector ran to get the water.

Hector handed the gourd to James, who set it down on the porch. He dipped his handkerchief in the water and lightly mopped Cordelia's brow, then with his fingers let tiny drops of water fall on her dry lips.

James Few was a hearty yet humble soul. He lived for the aspiration of bettering the quality of life for whomever he encountered; he never seemed to think on himself. His brown hair was curly and thick. He kept it cropped at medium length, not quite enough to tie at the nape as was the custom. His brown eyes were a near match for his hair color, and his ruddy face balanced the color scheme.

James was a man of average height and larger than average musculature, quick and adept and tireless. As a youth he reveled in sport and games of an athletic nature, ever buoying others up with his kind spirit and winsome smile. But the toil and care of making his place in the world, compounded with Fanning's clever wrecking of his life in

TURNER

daily increments, had seemed to erode the spark of joy from his demeanor until the generous smiles had slipped away to older times.

Still, deep within the recesses of his chained heart, a spark of good intent would never fully die; he would somehow manage to conjure a kind word or fleeting, faint smile when spoken to. The weight of oppression, though restrictive of internal good, nevertheless allowed some virtue to squeeze out from the sides once in a while.

Cordelia began to revive as Fanning explained to the sheriff, "This man made unwelcomed advances toward my servant!" Both James and Cordelia made incredulous expressions at Fanning, as James helped her into a sitting position.

"Well, I'll swanny! How can ye spin such a tale?" squeaked Cordelia.

"What an evil lie, Colonel! You know I came to her assistance!" James joined in. Then looking at his beloved Cordelia, he continued, "Come away with me, Cordie! I can find work at my uncle's smithy in Savannah, and we can be married!"

"See what I mean, Sheriff?" Fanning countered, with a faint, evil grin on his lips. "She's indentured. The thief!"

"Cordie, pack ye some things, and let us go away!" James urged.

"Do you forget this wench is bound to my estate until she is free of debt, Few?" Fanning snarled. His nose seemed to rise continually higher in the air. "And as for yourself, well, you are no longer needed in my employ. Furthermore, the ten pounds due on your account is payable in full—on the morrow! I would advise you not to remove anything from your land, as your property shall be forfeited to me, your creditor, pending appraisal by the court."

"Ye don't own everyone and everything, Fanning! And ye'll not determine if and when Cordie and I will be married!" James' usually amiable face tightened and quivered in desperation.

"Sheriff, escort this trespasser off my property!" The lawmen dismounted and seized James, who struggled until the deputy pistol-whipped him over the head. He

BLOOD AT ALAMANCE!

staggered in a daze while they bound him with a rope. Remounting, they led him off the plantation like livestock. Fanning pulled Cordelia back into the house by the arm. She shrieked so desperately that James and his captors could hear her through the walls.

James went wild with exasperation, yelling toward the house, "Run for it, Cordie! Meet me at the farm. Cordie! Cordie!" The lawmen spurred their horses on faster, causing James to trot behind them as they glanced grinningly back toward the wailing coming from the house.

CHAPTER FOUR

B　**ULLY** Billy Tryon had gotten his way. The North Carolina Assembly was coerced into voting approval for a new governor's palace. Then he bullied them into raising the budgeted allocation from 5,000 to 10,000 pounds, when the average colonial would be lucky to see a spare pound in a year.

The palace was an opulent brick structure akin to the Georgian style, situated on the Trent River. The gates swung from tall brick posts capped with stone spheres, and stood next to a brick pair of round guard shelters, each with narrow windows which also served as gunports. Wrought iron fences protruded thence, with vertical iron rods much like spears. The façade stood two stories high with several windows, its potentially austere appearance being tamed by the cream-colored paint of the large gable, in whose center was a splendid crest of gilded lions.

The spacious grounds were adorned with exquisite flowers and patterned shrubbery, and crowned with majestic native oaks. Expertly crafted paths paved with brick wove through the picturesque gardens, along which any resident would be pridefully confident in escorting the King, should he design to visit the manor. Though desiring grandeur in all respects, Tryon actually cared little for horticulture or garden plans, leaving the designer to struggle with the scheme for weeks until finally approving the landscaping. Still, foreign travelers would come to admire the grounds to the point that they would take sketches back to their own countries to introduce to their countrymen of wealth and influence.

Tryon would spend less time walking the garden paths, however, than he would walking the floors of his palace, looking down from the windows to observe how others were being impressed with their grandeur. Occasionally

BLOOD AT ALAMANCE!

one could see his portly figure gazing from his personal guard stations, always distinguishable by his rotund but sternly erect figure, with or without his white wig. His hair, graying into a blend of black and steel-gray, was loose and thinning. There was just enough for his valet to brush it back and tie it at the nape before setting his wig in place. His round face bore the image of having been well-fed.

Excesses of walking, or speech-making, or of any manner of exertion, would send little rivulets of perspiration along the furrows in his brow until they ran down the sides of his face, where they channeled off through the deepening wrinkles on either side of his mouth. His pallor only took color when he was exerting or in a verbal rage. His physique spoke of earlier times when he was a muscular young soldier, but now betrayed his life of ease.

When he had addressed the Assembly on the palace budget issue, he had come armed with every manipulative device in his political arsenal, determined to cajole, sweet-talk, or strong-arm them into granting his desires. Assuming the stand that day, he gripped the sides of the podium, looked over the gathered body, and seemed to visually inspect every individual face as though to intimidate them. Breathing steadily and peering up at the ceiling, then downward to the floor, a nervous presence began to build within the hall until bonding all present into one mutual state of apprehension. Following several intensified moments, Tryon raised his head to stare ahead is if deep in contemplation, seeming to calculate every minute aspect of the common mood. Once he sensed he had created a collective ambiance, he began to apply his verbal mastery.

"Loyal subjects of His Majesty King George, honorable Assembly, gentlemen, and friends," he burst out at last. Then with a softened tone he continued, "Well have we achieved a great milestone in the dignity of our Royal Colony, in the near-completion of the palace proper. I say *near*-completion for, although I reside therein now, we have issues yet to discuss. Sorely perplexing issues."

Following another calculated pause, he slapped the podium and began to rant, "But how dare we endeavor to

TURNER

present such affrontery to His Majesty, in the form of an official governmental residence devoid of the necessities to operate and sustain it in an honorable fashion! Know ye not that I represent His Majesty in all aspects of our colonial governance? Why then am I to be housed without the adjunct support of said house? Where are the outbuildings? Stables? Smithy? A carriage shop, a solarium, or a cottage retreat for intellectual pursuits? There is need for servants' quarters, tool and equipment buildings, and storehouses. This worthy project was approved in 1766. Now here it is 1771, and I have only resided in the edifice for one year. Moreover, it is still not in acceptable condition!"

Now gripping the podium as if intending to choke it, he slowly unflexed, softened his voice, and after a moment of quiet, went on. "I will leave it to you, then, gentlemen, to do the right thing, without delay. The budget allocation must be increased to ten thousand pounds, *and*..." Tryon jabbed a finger at the Assembly, then with a brief stern glimpse toward his Council, and finished with "...I say, *shall* be increased by vote *today!* Consider well your positions and responsibilities, all ye present. Mind ye well the course ye are now set upon." With this he turned about, vacated the stand, and stepped down the hallway into his office. Removing his wig, he withdrew a handkerchief from his sleeve with which to mop his brow in privacy.

Mrs. Tryon was seated in his office, arrayed in finery from her gilt-and-lace trimmed hat, to the hem of her designer dress. Every inch of fabric in between was the finest of golden Chinese silk accentuated with Belgian lace ruffling in abundance. Tryon stopped cold and suddenly speechless. With her gloves in one hand she slapped them against the other as if applauding.

"Well, hoorah for you!" she quipped with a smirk. Or should I rather say, "Bully for Bully Billy!" She made a teasing sideways glance and sarcastic little smile. *"Consider well— mind ye well!* All who hear those words know of what you speak—of the threat you portend."

He broke his momentary silence quickly enough. "Whatever are you doing here!" he demanded. Then with a softened tone and weasel-eyed manipulation, he coaxed, "That is—whatever are you doing here, my dear Margaret? This is no place for a woman! Especially a..."

"Were you this rejecting of your mother, also, William? Where would you be without the women in your life? A pompous, penniless pensioner."

Mrs. Tryon's brownish-red hair, usually close to her head and gathered in the back, was today styled to such fullness that it almost extended to the ends of her broad-brimmed hat. Pinned with combs of gold and pearl, the adornments of her coiffure alone were worth more than an average colonial could expect to earn in several lifetimes. Her earrings repeated the fashion of the combs, while her necklace of sizeable, perfect pearls was strung together with pure gold thread.

She was tall and overly slender, and had a face of fairness bordering on pale, accentuating her chestnut brows and tinted lips. Her cheeks, nose, and chin were elegantly styled as if chiseled by a discerning sculptor. Her high forehead and tall neck gave her the appearance of looming over those with whom she spoke, which she often used—along with her icy elegance and quipping aristocratic diction—to advantage, in persuading Tryon to her point of view.

So cool natured was she that she bore the look of a stone statue attempting to emerge into human form. Yet her heart was not without passion; her emotions were merely calculated and never wasted. She was born to high social stratum, and enjoyed richness and fineries long before Tryon had courted and married her; she was not at all dependent on his ill-gotten gains. Rather, he was dependent upon her rich dowry, which spurred him onward to desire an ever-increasing bounty of lucre of his own device.

"My dear, between my governing this Royal Colony and maintaining you in finery, I have more than enough pangs within my head than I can usually deal with. What would attract you to this unattractive aspect of a man's domain?"

With the slightest smirk, as if he were not worthy of her full reaction, she simply retorted, "Maintaining me? I doubt fame, fortune, or function would be well in hand for you, William, were it not for me. He jerked his head backward and grunted. "But I will leave you to your—*undertakings*. Though please, if it can be conceived within your ambitious mind, consider not taking more than Carolina can give. Eventually there will be no more to take. If you try to milk a dry cow, she may kick you in the face!"

But her words fell on stony ears. Though he had been in his palace for a year, Tryon would continue mercilessly to browbeat the Assembly for funds to lavishly furnish and richly maintain his luxurious lair. It became his one principal obsession. Assemblymen and other officials, fearing for their fortunes—and sometimes their very lives—always came forth with an increase in over-taxation and outright extortion of the colonists, to the point that this became a way of life among them.

Tryon with his lapdog Governor's Council, all handpicked, essentially controlled the Assembly. There were five representatives from each coastal county and two from each rural county, each of whom had a voice in the Assembly, but who easily came under retribution if their words were not aligned with the whims and wishes of Tryon.

Assemblyman Herman Husband, a rare adherent to political honesty with a common sense approach to government, was a troublesome stone in the stream for Tryon's navigation of his every scheme. Although he had been practically thrown out of the Assembly, Herman continued to protest to the point that Tryon made it his personal campaign to have him humiliated and annihilated swiftly as possible. Before Robert Messer embarked on his short pilgrimage to Alamance, Tryon had met with Edmund Fanning to discuss the very subject.

"What of that backwoods ballyhoo, Husband!" Tryon had ranted. "He was freed from jail by a gang of armed traitors!"

Fanning, looking out the window at the fine gardens below, interjected, "True sir, a treasonous throng went forth to free him, but the judge declared him innocent of libel

BLOOD AT ALAMANCE!

against you and released him, shortly before they arrived." He turned toward Tryon. "Another instead was charged with the libel charge against Your Excellency, and…" His flowing words froze suddenly, upon seeing Tryon turning red and clinching his fists.

"Blast you, Fanning! Husband needs jailing at all times, for any number of charges. He and Rednap Howell have woven together a large body of rebels who now refuse to even pay their taxes! This you know. Or surely should!"

"Yes, Governor. As you say." Fanning felt himself hewn to the floor in one fell blow, and began to inwardly rebuild himself as he bowed in humble obeisance.

Bully Billy, with the bellowing voice of a wild bovine, strode up and down in his office chambers sputtering to Fanning about this thorn in his hide. Fanning, his aspiring protégé and partner in corruption, was a ready audience.

"They shall meet an untimely demise, yet in the most timely manner!" Fanning replied with a cold sneer. His outward confidence betrayed his inward fear, gulping from the lie he had presented to Tryon. He let Tryon go on believing that Husband was freed from jail in Hillsborough on legal grounds, but the seventy or so armed farmers who came to his rescue had actually influenced the decision—a decision rendered by Fanning himself. Fanning had actually granted him sudden bail on learning of the mob's approach, on the condition that Husband would state no further "jealousy" over Fanning's officers "executing their lawful duties," e.g., extorting their outrageous fees. Husband feigned compliance with Fanning's confessed intent to continue his crimes, then skipped about the country resuming his organization of the Regulator Movement.

Tryon calmed himself momentarily, and continued with his obsession over Herman Husband. "Timing is the word, you see. For beyond these criminals, Husband has a strong general following, and they are, more often than not, congregating about him."

"When we begin to collect the palace maintenance dues, they'll fail him soon enough. Already I have a scheme to implicate Husband's followers for bribery, thievery, conspiracy, and..."

"Oh, come away from it, man! No scheming will be needed. For when we press for the palace treasury, these backwoodsmen will scurry like squirrels to raise their due, and hence protect their homes and holdings, leaving Mr. Husband quite undefended."

"What they are able to retain of them." Fanning revived his sinister sneer.

"Now see here, Edmund. You were to exact by whatever means necessary from your county's constituency, any and all hard cash that exists—keep the money flowing into our coffer, while reducing the colonials to mere subsistence and reliance upon their land and farm produce. Money is power, and they needn't have any."

"True, they have no real need for currency anyway. Or they shan't, once it is only a memory." Fanning beamed at His Excellency's referring to him as Edmund now.

"Nor power, man. *Power!* What would they do with it? Wreck the colony. Ruin life as we know it." Tryon held out his two fists and made a motion like breaking a stick. "You have failed to keep order in Orange County! Judge Henderson has been driven from the bench and the sheriff can no longer enforce writs or summonses without your own militiamen interfering! And now your rebels are refusing to pay any more taxes!"

Fanning propped his left elbow atop the mantel, right fist on hip, left hand waving about as he spoke, effecting an air of sophistication. "Monetary means are meant for those born to it. But even a pig resists one's taking his apple, once it falls from limb to sty."

"Marketable goods that can be converted to ready cash shall be the second order of business. But first and foremost, the currency. We must have the palace completed in order to attract and entice His Majesty to committing himself to a Royal visit to our fair colony."

"And of course, lesser dignitaries, marketers, and..."

"And those who can—shall we say—enhance and benefit the colony!"

"To the King; may his glory reign in Carolina!"

BLOOD AT ALAMANCE!

"To the King! And may his glory *rain* down upon us!"

The two conspirators toasted their sovereign, while outside the doorway a black manservant knocked, then entered, announcing, "Your Excellency, Captain Wilcox."

"Come in, come in, Captain," Tryon gestured.

Wilcox was brisk for business, and had the full attention of the Governor. He hurried across the floor in a military manner and started to hand him a written message, but hesitated upon noting Fanning's presence.

"Come, Captain. Your report. The Colonel is privy to matters of State," Tryon said, stretching out his hand to receive the dispatch. Fanning sneered at Wilcox with narrowed eyes and lips, in defiance of this lower ranked officer whom he felt had just snubbed him. Tryon read in earnest silence, then continued, "Thank you, Captain! That will be all!" He slammed the paper together as if an internal thunder had manifested itself through his hands.

"It's Husband!" Tryon bellowed. "He has been seen on the Goldsboro Road, heading northwest. Talk is, that he is bound for Alamance, to incite an uprising—in *your* county, Edmund!" His anger smoothed over like a calming tide of soothing waters, as he continued, "He is exactly where we want him—right in the midst of those upcountry rebels!"

"Then I must ride! There is much to attend there!" Fanning deduced, hoping to retain hometown autonomy.

"We must all ride! The Assembly has approved my campaign plans. We march at once! Ah, the example we shall make of one Herman Husband, Esquire, there amongst those whose minds he has tainted against us!"

"If only we still had time to incite the Indians against those—those *Regulators*, as they style themselves. Let the Indians clean them off the land, as we had hoped."

"Now Edmund, you had sufficient time for that endeavor. But the game is far gone. And afterward, we would only have to reclaim the land from the Indians—*again*—from they who do not pay taxes!"

Aides were summoned; orders were shouted through the palace and out onto the lawn. The Governor's Militia was forming up and outfitting for a campaign. Tryon hastily dictated a proclamation suspending the sale of lead and gunpowder in all counties west and north of New Bern.

"We shall march without drums. We shall undertake a forced march, catch them unawares, and give them a taste of their own deviltry!" Tryon declared to Fanning. Fanning gripped the handle of his sword, looking out the window with a cunning grin at the militiamen below, some in Redcoat uniforms, but mostly clad in common garb, distinguished mainly by their black leggings and yellow cockades on their black tricorner hats. He looked upon opportunity for exploitation as a planter would look over his crops.

Tryon's army marched with 300 men on April 24, 1771. By May 1, his ranks had been greatly reinforced by militiamen drawn from every county along the way. On May 4, they encamped by the Eno River.

Those militiamen from the western counties who would reluctantly comply, received their orders to report to Salisbury to join ranks under Gen. Hugh Waddel. There they would encamp until ready to march to Hillsborough to join Tryon.

Waddel's camp daily witnessed despondent militiamen reporting in, spirits sagging from Tryon's extortions, and further weighted down from rumors that they were to march on their own people—the Regulators who were striving to save their very existence. Despite his high rank and lofty command, Waddel was not able to raise more than a small company of men over several days.

Two young militiamen from Orange County were sent out to gather firewood for the camp. "Did ye hyar about Old Man Reedy?" asked one.

"Burnt him out, them devils. Robbed everything he had. But he escaped," replied his young comrade.

"Well, I heered Butler's men catched up with him and hung him by the road. Left him a-danglin' thar, fer all to see! Never done nary a thang to harm man ner beast!"

His young friend dropped his armload of sticks and fell to his knees. His eyes welled up with tears as he silently uttered a prayer.

BLOOD AT ALAMANCE!

Their sergeant approached on foot and shouted, "Back to it, now, boys! Leftenant's a-comin', directly!"

"I'll never fight for Waddel," the boy said to his fellow trooper as he helped him to his feet. "What about you?" He answered with a wag of the head, and a vacant, bemused look that spoke on behalf of his failing words.

A shipment of gunpowder was en route from Charleston to Gen. Waddel at his Salisbury camp. A lone soldier with a bandage tied about his head rode hard and fast into camp, and dismounted at Waddel's tent.

"I must see the General immediately," he said with great anxiety, elbowing past sentries and saluting several staff officers.

Waddel waved his entourage aside and asked calmly, "What is your report, Sergeant?"

The rider saluted and announced, "A band of Cabarras County men overran the gunpowder convoy, sir, between Charlotte and Salisbury!"

Amidst the gasping and growling of his staff, Waddel inquired, "What's become of it, then?"

"The guard were all wounded, or dispersed. A couple were kilt. Then the powder, all of it, was burnt!"

The General's countenance quickly dulled with disappointment. Astonished faces looked on as he further asked, "Were any of these rebels identifiable?"

"Sir, they had all blackened their faces."

"How do you know of a certainty, they were Cabarras men? And how do you alone survive, to report?"

"Sir, I fired on them, then fought with all my might. I was clubbed by a musket barrel, and fell to the ground. Seeing the guard had all gone down or fled, I feigned death until the attackers left. But I heard one of them say, 'Huzzah for Cabarras!' After they left, I found one of our horses and rode straight here."

"Give him rest and rations," Waddel remarked, patting him on the shoulder. Then turning away, he ordered his staff, "Dispatch a small detail to locate and tend to the wounded. Prepare to advance. Our present powder stores will have to suffice."

TURNER

"But sir, can we send a detachment to hunt down the saboteurs?" asked a colonel.

"We cannot be distracted from our orders. We shall rendezvous with General Tryon post haste. The matter will be his to resolve."

On May 10, Waddel's forces forded the Yadkin River, re-inspected their gear, accounted for men and beasts, and prepared to press onward toward Hillsborough. But there were noticeably fewer men in their ranks after the crossing, and desertions increased with every mile.

Soon a large party of Regulators emerged from the forest under a flag of truce, and stopped Waddel's column. They met with only a trace of resistance: once the militiamen saw their white flag, and no doubt recognized some of them as neighbors and Regulators, they were relieved to return their muskets to their shouldered positions.

"General Waddel and company," called out one of the men. "These lands are now under the watch of the Regulators. You will turn your men about, and retreat!" Waddel exchanged blank stares with his staff officers. Seeing even more of his men leave the column, he gestured with his head to turn about, and they began to reverse the column.

Encouraged by the retreat, several Regulators began to shatter the quiet of the forest with whoops of triumph, which spurred the mob into a screaming charge. Waddel's company beat a hasty retreat and crossed back over the Yadkin. The Regulators pursued even past the river, surrounding the remnant of Waddel's followers. Some of them set up a defensive stance and fired on the Regulators, who swiftly overpowered them with returned fire and manual combat.

Waddel and a few of his men escaped and fled back to Salisbury. The remaining captives were disarmed, their food and supplies divided by half, and were ordered to disperse in many directions.

The practices of this body of Regulators were not entirely in unison with those of the greater number, who sought peaceful, lawful redress of the gross injustices so besetting them. Armed assault was particularly detested

BLOOD AT ALAMANCE!

and resisted by their mentors, Herman Husband and Rednap Howell. But in the spirit of their cause, they were bound and unified. And though the Royal government may not have recognized it at this early stage, nor even the oppressed colonials, a revolution was in the making; and from these bold sparks a cleansing fire of reform was eager to sweep the land.

By May 13, word of Waddel's disastrous retreat had reached Tryon. He swiftly mobilized his forces and crossed the Haw River, advancing toward the objective of Alamance.

CHAPTER FIVE

BACK in Orange County, Sheriff Butler kept dogging the trail of Jamison Ledford, who had been freed from his treacherous snare by sympathetic passersby. These men represented a reactionary element found within the ranks of the otherwise peaceful and loosely structured Regulators, whose actions were gaining popularity.

Herman Husband was the undying voice and spirit of the Regulator Movement, inspiring the colonials to appeal peacefully to the Governor for a legal and equitable solution to the many injustices they suffered. When a few of the men took the law into their own hands, Herman made every effort to rein in their exuberance. Yet in the eyes of the Governor, these errant few exemplified the entire movement, casting them all as outlaws to be dealt with severely, despite Tryon's having crushed all peaceable efforts. Thus Tryon was forcing increasing numbers of Regulators to consider Herman's pacifist ways obsolete.

Further up the road, half a dozen of these frustrated Regulators sat talking on the porch of Aaron Stonecypher, seething with rage as he told them of Butler's abuse of his new wife. These community comrades were good men of the Earth, solid in their constitution and ever committed to their sense of right. They well represented the current generation of survivors of the demanding land, austere in their bearing yet true to their fellowman; theirs was a degree of devotion Tryon, Fanning, or Butler could not begin to comprehend. They were the actual strength of the colony and of America, and indeed of every land where the common folk bear the burden of civilization's survival. They were born to survive and raised to help their neighbors survive. This day they sat whitling, inspecting their

BLOOD AT ALAMANCE!

firearms, petting their hounds—until gradually their tempers came to the boiling point as they began to disregard their superficial amusements, and to focus on Aaron's livid discourse on treachery coming so close to home.

Today the bond of brotherhood began to tighten all the more, as Aaron proclaimed, "They made me pay five pounds for an extree marriage license! Don't see that much in a year! Just the few things 'round here was all I owned, in the world! And Armilia and I had barely got home from the weddin'," he lamented, "afore Butler and his mob pounded on the door. Says he, *'Since ye ain't married in the Church o'England, there be a new tax upon ye of five pounds.'* Well, I didn't have it about me, so they took my gun, plow, and mule, and then made Armilia take off her new dress at gunpoint, for public sale!"

Aaron's accounts put the men into a rage. The tension was so sudden and potent that men gasped aloud, dropped their whittling, and seized their guns and knives with steely grips as the ever-perceptive hounds yelped and darted several feet away at the unexpected mass excitement. This was their breaking point. "Butler's day has nigh come!" one man commented, his words seething like flames.

"*Has* come, ye *mean!*" said another.

"What'll hit be, men? Gun, knife, or rope?" growled Elisha Roland, a natural leader among them.

"Put the law on him," replied another.

"What law? What law?" the men shouted in unison.

"We will have to be the law!" answered Roland.

On the Salisbury Road between Hillsborough and Alamance, Sheriff Butler and his men met Thaddeus Ledford, owner of the horse they had attempted to seize from his brother Jamison. Thaddeus smiled and nodded at the men, then on realizing who they were, gasped in wide-eyed horror and spurred his horse to a gallop. Shots were fired toward him as his superior horse—so envied by Butler—easily pulled away from the lawmen's mounts.

First Butler, then Jep and Broley, spurred their horses and took out after him. A furious race ensued, as dirt and pebbles from the road began to fly.

TURNER

The gunshots alerted the Regulators on the Stonecypher porch, inspiring them to mount and chase after the action. Neither they nor the lawmen ever suspected that Herman Husband was coming toward them, who, on hearing gunshots and thundering hoofs, reined his horse quickly into the concealment of the bushes. As the galloping uproar was passing him, Herman recognized some of the Regulators who were in hot pursuit. He whistled loudly at them. They reined up, looked back up the road, and saw him signaling from the bushes. Riding up to greet their mentor Herman, they were dismayed at his disapproving countenance.

"Why, Brother Herman..." began Roland, eagerly. "I liked not to have knowed ye!"

"Brother indeed," replied Herman, clearly displeased. "What 'brotherly' endeavor are ye about, dare I ask?"

"Why, Brother Herman," began another. "Sheriff Butler has seized an innocent man—Thaddeus Ledford—all for naught! And is bound to work his misery on him!"

"Hit's Fanning's doing. And Tryon's! Robbing him in the name of put-on taxes!" enjoined yet another.

"Come to meeting on the morrow. Thou knowest the place. Up Salisbury Road. I have prepared another written appeal to the Governor, which we Regulators may now deliver to him as a united body."

"Another'un?" Roland replied, the others reacting with supportive shouts and nods. "T'won't do much more'n the last one, seems to me like."

"I admonish thee, put aside the urge for vengeance, as it will come to naught. There is a higher course, and we must pursue it."

Herman resumed his journey up the road while the agitated men met in council, their words humming with the energy that derives from oppression working its way through the cracks. Turning to see that Herman was out of sight, they collectively spurred their horses on down the road toward Hillsborough.

Thaddeus looked for opportunities amongst the thick brush on the roadsides, to leave the common path and lose his pursuers in the woods. Before he could, he saw

BLOOD AT ALAMANCE!

Roland and his Regulators riding toward him in a frenzied gallop. Thinking they, too, were in pursuit of him, he wheeled his horse about and took off back down the road, visually scanning the bushes for an opportune opening.

Rounding a bend, suddenly Butler and his men came into view. Spinning about in the road in confused frustration, he was soon surrounded by his adversaries. They drew their pistols and leveled them at him. Butler chided, "At last! Come home to roost, have ye?" Butler motioned with his head and pistol for Thaddeus to ride on back toward Hillsborough.

They rode easily for a hundred yards past the bend, when the sound of racing hoofs caused the lawmen to turn about and see the raging Regulators. Butler whipped the back of Thaddeus' horse with his horse's reins and yelled, "Hyah!" The four raced on toward town.

"They done took Thad agin!" yelled Roland. The Regulators intensified their dispatch in hot pursuit.

Recklessly scaring people off the streets with their hasty arrival in town, Butler and his deputies rapidly dismounted and led Thaddeus up the courthouse steps and on up the staircase, eager to have him arraigned without delay. The Regulators entered, stormed up the stairs, and tore him away from the three lawmen.

"Run for it, Thad!" cried one.

"Make your escape now, Thad! Your horse is still tied out front!" cried another.

The six Regulators, energized by the cause of truer justice, easily overpowered Butler and his men. Hurling them to the floor, they dragged them all down the stairs by the heels, banging their heads on each step. With futility the magistrate wielded his gavel, pounding out a near-echo of the banging sounds cascading down the courthouse stairs.

Thaddeus stood in awe of the sudden mayhem. A man of peace himself, he was unaccustomed to the practice of taking action against lawless lawmen. But once the magistrate shouted for the bailiff to seize him, he soon found himself bounding down the stairs amongst the mob, and sprinting toward his horse. The steed reared and

TURNER

whirled about until he gained control of the reins and prodded him down the road, jumping fences and blazing new trails across pastures and meadows until disappearing in the woods.

Butler shouted, "'Tis Fanning's doing! Fanning ordered the arrest! Turn us a-loose and take your case to him!"

The Regulators eyed Butler and each other for one intensive moment, then Roland growled, "Fanning, eh! Here, let's tether Fanning's pups to the post, and pay the Colonel a call!"

The mob shouted unanimous approval.

"But first a little taste of what's in store for these buzzards!" Roland continued. He removed his belt and yelled, "Let's whup the feathers off of them!" He began to whip the three bound men. The other five joined in the action until the ruckus was broken by a lady screaming across the street. They remounted and turned up the road, hurling threats and epithets toward Butler and his men: "Black-hearted devils!"—"Woman-beaters!"—"Ye'll get the rope yet!"

Riding hard and fast toward Fanning Plantation, they were as disappointed at not finding him at home, as they had been with finding Butler carrying out his misdeeds.

"Let's torch the place!" cried Roland. "Just like they did his town house last year!"

The other men shook their heads and mumbled discouragements. Simmons said, "No, too much risk for us, and our folks. Fanning won't stop until he's hung everybody in the land!"

Roland reflected a moment, frowning. Then with a crusty grin he offered, "I reckon he needs a little roof work, fellows. I see a nail a-working loose up yonder. I'll drive it back in for him!" With a grin, he shouldered his musket and shot a hole in Fanning's roof. "Hmm. Must've missed. I'll try'er again." As he reloaded, the remaining five followed suit, drilling holes in the wood shingles which would give Fanning something to think about when the next rain came. Their deed done, they turned about and raced their horses on back up the road from whence they had come.

BLOOD AT ALAMANCE!

Their derring-do was not typical of American colonials, living under the strong arm of the Royal government. But equally atypical were the peaceful, albeit resistive, meetings conducted by Herman Husband. The spirit of rebellion was manifesting itself in many forms, to varying degrees. But the spirit was growing nonetheless.

A great deal of it had to do with the sense of individual independence the colonials developed by having to survive off the land, relying on their own industry, imagination, and faith. And as the hand of oppression came down ever harder, the spirit was not smothered, because it was too alive and held so in earnest by the common folk of upcountry North Carolina. Rather, that spirit of liberty was beginning to squirm from beneath that heavy hand, even to dodge its ever-falling blows.

The upcountry was also ripe for budding democracy, being largely settled by discontents from Royalist-influenced Virginia, as well as independent-minded Scots and Irish coming south, and Germans from the coast, in quest of new lands. Tryon, in his shortsighted view from his ivory tower of self-delusion, could only see their resources, not their hearts.

Tryon, after all, was a man of mercenary means. Abandoning his wife and their daughter, he married London heiress Margaret Wake and her £30,000 dowry. This nuptial merger also propelled him from Captain to Leftenant Colonel, and eventually to General. His fortune and career were set. Yet he was never satisfied without more—more of everything that was not already his.

Tryon was not on Robert Messer's mind as he arose refreshed in the home of Jason and Harriett Caldwell, where he had stayed the night. But he did come to mind as Robert prayed on his knees a considerable spell for the future of his family and neighbors; and for the cause of right, on which errand he earnestly perceived himself this day.

Having soon breakfasted and exchanged morning niceties with the Caldwells, he stepped out to the porch to await the arrival of men from his militia company. Jason

TURNER

hobbled up, leaned on his carved poplar cane, and joined him in conversation.

"Are you mustering the entire company?" Jason queried.

"No, we're not mustering. Just inviting as many as may want to come to meeting. Hit's not a militia action. Just friends and neighbors, common folk who want relief from the present tyranny. Just aiming to talk over the next course of action."

"Do ye think Herman Husband is really a-comin'?"

"I surely do. On his word of honor, he intends to, leastways."

"Sha, after Tryon arrested him, and then them fellers sprung him out of jail, I allowed he'd be a-layin' low by this time!"

"I pray to Heaven he is safe! But I do trust he will make every effort to be here, as promised."

"What d'ya think he'll do, 'xactly? Stir up some action?"

Robert glanced sideways at Jason, then back toward the road, shaking his head. "No. He will speak of peace, and peaceful solutions. I imagine he'll tame the passion of those hearts that long for violence, yet fire up many a heart to the higher cause of God-given rights—and continue to appeal for harmony through peace."

"But if Tryon means to give us the bayonet, what then?"

Robert grinned and shook his head again, looking squarely at Jason. "I'm certain we'll hear more than one point of view, 'fore hit's over."

"So, nary a chance of action? Taking the Bully by the horns?"

"Well, I never said that." Robert looked at his musket leaning against the wall by the door.

"Wish to Heaven I could accompany you'uns." He patted his bad leg. "Ye'll have to bring me a full report of the happenings."

"If I don't, hit'll be because..."

"Look'ee, men are a-coming up the road now."

BLOOD AT ALAMANCE!

Men continued to trickle into the Caldwell yard, exchanging salutations with Robert and with one another. The gathering broke out into a dozen small conversational groups, making the tree leaves hum with eager talk about events that had occurred, and those possibly awaiting them.

Robert retrieved his horse from the stable and was soon back on the road. He again enjoyed the morning May sun as it filtered through the canopy of trees, massaging his face and invigorating his spirits. He pondered how such a simple pleasure could be so uplifting, even treasured, particularly when the thought arose that it may be a fleeting pleasure depending on the outcome of the actions to which he was now committed.

He retrieved Herman's pamphlet from his breast pocket and began to read it again, thoughtfully pondering every word and phrase, and silently hoping—praying—that Herman's pen would indeed be mightier than the sword, and effectuate an appreciable degree of frontier justice. As Robert contemplated those enlightening thoughts of peace, again two sinister figures from the darker dimension of colonial life observed him and his companions intently from the woods, noting his direction and pace as he wound his way toward Herman's meeting.

A distant neighbor, Alvin Spivey, recognized Robert and nudged his horse up alongside him and Atticus.

"You see 'em, Cap'n Messer?" asked the rider, a man well past middle age, soft in muscle and dumpy enough to practically bond with his horse and saddle in one unison of movement, yet tan and rugged enough to suggest he still had some years of toughness left in him. His raspy voice echoed years of observation of frontier colonial life; keen but calm; perhaps almost sing-songy in his lilt in younger years, until the vocal chords began to age.

Keeping his eyes straight ahead, Robert replied matter-of-factly, "Yes, I see them, Mr. Spivey. They've been spying all along, ever since I left home yesterday."

"Butler's men, no doubt."

"His, or Fanning's. Or both."

TURNER

"What could they want of you—of any of us?" The senior gent's croaky voice peeled through the morning mist and fluttered like an old bird.

"Until now, I was more concerned with joining up with our neighbors and seeing our cause through. Maybe I should've thought more on Butler's threats."

The old man turned toward Robert with a start. "Butler after ye, too, now?"

"Isn't he after everybody?" Robert resumed the rereading of Herman's pamphlet and let Atticus plod gently on.

"Well," the old man warbled on, "hit's too purdee a day to think about the likes of them fellers. Or the things they could do to ruin it."

Robert's concentration again became absorbed into the leaflet, but soon he was distracted from his reading as traffic on the old dirt road increased: men astride horses, and many afoot. Only a very few could afford carriages. As they drew nearer to Alamance, the trickle of men grew to be a throng; men come to represent the strength of the common folk; men called Regulators, for to regulate the affairs of runaway local government was their principal aim.

The men, some 2,000 strong, began to assemble in the church yard of the Quaker Meeting House along Salisbury Road. Men of every age, some of modest means, some poor and others poorer—some with faces reflecting refinement while others revealed the haggard evidence of harsh frontier life—all stood shoulder to shoulder, bound by the spirit of humanity and true brotherhood. The fires of tyranny had wrought the finest of gold in their hearts, welding a sure bond of righteous determination. All carried muskets, as was the custom of frontier survival. But they had not assembled as an armed force.

Three Quaker men worked their way through the crowd, one calling, "Brother Herman, know thee not this is a place of peace?"

"Fear not, Brethren," Herman calmly replied. "We are here today to promote peace—the Lord's peace."

BLOOD AT ALAMANCE!

A momentary distraction was created with the arrival of a splendid carriage drawn by a horse of superior breeding, the property of an obviously affluent gentleman being driven by his black manservant.

The attention of the crowd soon turned to watch as a humble but dignified gentleman of middle age climbed into the bed of a wagon in the church yard, and stood looking over the congregation. A sudden hush swept the crowd as he withdrew papers from the breast pocket of his coat, and prepared to speak.

CHAPTER SIX

WISDOM'S very essence, carried on wings of peace, flowed with the soul-searching words of Herman Husband. If no man present lived beyond May 15, 1771, he could go to his grave with the satisfaction that he and his countrymen had a voice among them of inspiration and power—and the power to make inspired thoughts truly live within their breasts. Within his words rang a gentle but sure reminder that Right was still alive, if only within their hearts. But if alive, it could grow, and liberty and dignity might just be attainable one day.

"Sons of Heaven," Herman began, "and brothers of the land: today we have gathered to bring forth a change, by faith with good works, in the wellbeing of our people. Seeds we plant today may not yield a ready harvest for our day, but will surely continue to prosper in the nurturance of Heaven's sunlight, until a day when our children, yea, and our children's children, will be able to walk with their heads erect and fear the scorn and abuse of no man."

"Amen, amen," hummed among the crowd like a common spirit, as Herman went on.

"Let us so live, that our God will prosper our good works, and that our seed shall remember us in our day as those who stood for liberty, justice, and dignity. May our model be such that our seed shall cling to it, cherish it, and never again in the history of the human race abandon our God-given rights!"

Applause and cheers erupted, stilled only by Herman's upraised hand and gently shaking head.

"Liberty! Humanity!" some men began to chant, while others called out, "God-given rights!" The words of freedom and respect for mankind seemed to have no relevance to the two black slaves among the crowd; one a farm hand and the other a coachman for the one

BLOOD AT ALAMANCE!

affluent gentleman in attendance. But Herman seemed sensitive to their plight, in the face of the irony of his sincere words.

Herman could not resist casting a brief, pitying eye toward the enslaved men, both of whom let their eyes sink downward as if to say that his words had, indeed, struck a chord within their bosoms; words they were not allowed to register upon their faces.

"Let the God of mercy shower down the rays of freedom upon *all* men within his creations, by and by," Herman continued. "To obey just laws, or to live in slavery, are two entirely different matters!"

The affluent man, listening from his carriage, reached forward and tapped his black coachman with his cane and said, "We've heard enough, Old Henry. Let us return home." The driver slapped the reins and turned the horse and carriage about in the dirt lane, and headed homeward with his master. The commoner men stood back and gave ground, watching in silence as the well-dressed master left their gathering. His driver was better attired than many of the white men in this assemblage.

"Reckon he's one of *them*?" said one man, jerking his head toward the departing carriage.

"A King's man?" replied another. "Or just a sheriff's man?"

"Why, that dandy goose, he'll probably go tell Fanning about our meetin'!" remarked another. "P'raps we orter go stop 'im!" The man hefted his musket from the ground, holding it up to view. Some of the other men, with accents ranging from Carolinian to Pennsylvanian, to Irish, Scottish, German, and British, echoed "Amen, yea, and aye!"

Robert shook his head and answered them all with the observation, "No, men. He only wanted to spare his servant from hearing the words we hold dear!"

The cackle began to cease, with some of the men looking toward Robert. Some seemed offended, as if Robert were promoting rights for blacks; while others silently expressed shame. But all eyes and ears soon turned again toward Herman, as he continued his speech.

TURNER

"Regulation, gentlemen. Regulation of tyranny is what we want, and is all we ask. We cannot expect the Garden of Eden to sprout for us overnight. We cannot expect a perfect existence was ever intended for the mortal sojourn through which we must struggle by trial and faith. But as creatures of the One True God, it is nevertheless incumbent upon us to stand for the right. We have no other recourse— we are forced to seek redress from the burdensome oppression about to doom us!"

"*Amen, yea, and aye!*" resonated again through the throng.

"The principal step, then, is to petition for regulation as an ever-swelling tide. The Governor has rebuked every written request for regulation, refused every plea to meet as honest gentlemen, and scandalized every request to be treated as human beings. Our tactful tide must never ebb."

The mild murmur of "Treason!" was heard to ripple worriedly through the crowd, followed by whisperings of "No, hear him out!"

Herman, cognizant of the concern being expressed by some, continued, "Let the spirit of treason be far from our souls. Rather, let us safeguard this day the Regulator Movement, with an eye to the sole objective of assisting His Honour, the Governor, in maintaining the respectability and safety intended for North Carolina by His Majesty, King George! Let no man stand for treason, but for inspired protection of our rights, families, and property!" Amidst thunderous applause, Herman doffed his hat and climbed down, humbly nodding and waving.

Various militia officers now congregated around the wagon. Robert was urged by them to mount the makeshift podium and address the gathering. He stood patiently looking over the mass of men, awaiting their buzzing conversations to subside. One by one, men noticed him atop the wagon, nudged his neighbor, and let the talk trickle to a stop.

"Men of Orange County and others hereabout— Rowan, Granville, Anson—neighbors—workers of the ground—good friends, and good Carolinians: This is not a military operation. But to organize ourselves as we march to

BLOOD AT ALAMANCE!

the Governor will put down a lot of confusion, and will help us better communicate amongst ourselves. I ask ye, if ye will, to assemble with your own militia companies, and to remain under the leadership of your captains until we have approached the Governor and concluded our business. Any among ye who are not part of a militia company, consider joining yourselves to the company of your friends, or form up as best ye can and follow the rest."

The various militia officers stood on the porch, on stumps, or sat on horseback, calling out to the men of their respective companies. As they began to gather as units, a horseman rode briskly into the scene. Reining up at the church yard, he called out, "Tryon has formed his army!"

Voices blared and feet shuffled about in excited turmoil. Once their noise ebbed, the rider continued, "He is marching on Hillsborough, with 1,200 men, plus cavalry and cannon!"

"Then hit'll be war!" shouted one man.

"Yes, give 'em battle!" cried another. Now hundreds of voices were again raised in thunderous threatening, while those of equal number urging peace were drowned out.

Herman remounted the wagon bed, waving his hat about until gaining the attention of the men once more.

"Now what are ye about, Brother Herman?" one of the Quakers called out. Herman nodded and answered, "Be at peace."

"Good neighbors!" he called out. "Christian men!"

"It's time to fight, Brother Herman!" called out one man. "Like Moses and Joshua. And David!"

"Good men, I pray it is not. My religion is the Society of Friends, whose meeting-house grounds are nigh desecrated with your blood-lust. Let us seek a peaceable solution!"

"But Herman, you tried that in the Assembly," cried one man.

The rider announced, "And, sir, Tryon seeks ye head by warrant! A bounty be on ye, and ye'd best take leave whilst ye can!"

"Then be gone, Herman!" urged Robert, lest any rogue amongst us take ye for a bounty!" Herman was swiftly escorted by several men towards his horse, and directed to leave through the woods. He was barely mounted when some of the men swatted his horse, causing it to leap into a gallop through the woods.

"It appears Brother Herman's work be done," remarked one man to Robert.

"Or, just beginning," Robert replied.

As the men resumed organizing themselves, a half dozen were dispatched in advance to spy out the situation in Hillsborough.

Tryon's Army had not yet broken camp outside Hillsborough. Tryon sat before his tent in red uniform beside Col. Fanning, enjoying a sumptuous breakfast.

"I daresay," remarked Fanning. "This fare is superior to the typical military rations one is accustomed to in camp."

Tryon lifted the napkin hanging on his chest, wiped his mouth and sneered, replying, "That is simply explained—because these are not rations, at least not for you and I. They are the fat of the land, foraged by my troops. One finds the farmers' goods hereabout quite ready for the taking—in the name of the King."

"To the King," answered Fanning, with a sneer to reflect Tryon's, holding high a fork-load of prime smoked ham.

Two mounted officers, Lt. Col. John Bautista Ashe and Captain John Walker, rode briskly up to Tryon's tent and reined in suddenly. Dismounting, Ashe rendered a salute and said with great excitement, "General Tryon, sir, if it so please—a message of greatest import."

"You may speak freely, Colonel," replied Tryon, shifting his fork to his left hand, then wiping his right hand on his napkin before returning the salute.

"Sir, the colonial rebels are formed and are in movement."

"Now?"

"Yes, sir. They are advancing on us in great numbers, bearing arms, and headed toward Alamance."

"Colonel Fanning, give the order to gather my staff officers, here. Immediately."

Fanning called out, "Bugler, sound Officers' Call!"

BLOOD AT ALAMANCE!

"Colonel Ashe, resume your reconnoitering," Tryon continued. "And report promptly and regularly. We shall make short work of this—this insolence!" Tryon sat back down to finish his feast.

Ashe and Walker rode away quickly toward Hillsborough Road to seek out the approach of the Regulators, and to determine their numbers and assets.

The advance spies scurried back on foot to the Regulators, reporting that Tryon's camp had apparently been alerted, and that the woods and roads were being reconnoitered by Tryon's forces.

In the absence of uniform leadership or consistent communication, the men began to bunch up and discuss the situation among themselves.

Comments filled the air like a flight of anxious birds, with voices eagerly uttering, "We're done for now"—"No, we have to commit to it"—"I'm bound for home"—"Well, I'll take a stand in Alamance!"—"We'll all hang for this"—"I'll march, but unarmed!"

Robert sat high atop his horse and cried out, "Men! Regulators! Hear me!" Hundreds of worried voices quieted, to hear the voice of one calm man. "We will march in numbers to show our unity. But we will not march as a presence of arms! Bring ye arms, or leave them by the way, but stand together and let us make our purpose known!"

Men began to nod and move forward, some hiding their muskets under leaves, in rocky clefts, and in the hollows of trees. As they advanced, only about half of them bore arms, and these mainly due to backcountry custom. Most carried no more powder or bullets than they would take on a brief hunt for small game.

A few curious onlookers along the way casually joined ranks with the Regulators, if only to tag along as observers. And it was rumored that a Captain Benjamin Merrill was advancing his own militia company from the south, to reinforce the Regulators. Many Tories in Orange County, though typically friendly toward Tryon, refused to get involved in any struggle against their Regulator neighbors. Thus the Regulators' hopes soared as they realized Tryon was going to be deep in unfriendly territory, with naught

TURNER

but Regulators and their friends surrounding the countryside.

As the mob neared Alamance, Lt. Col. Ashe and Capt. Walker were surprised by a band of Regulators, who captured them and pulled them from their horses. A few of the men who held personal grudges against Ashe and Walker bound them to trees and began to give them severe whippings with their belts.

"My brother was treated just so, by your men, Ashe!" cried one of the men, laying on the lashes severely.

"And you, Walker, you want to grow up to be a big woman beater like Fanning's men?" screamed another, whipping away with equal ferocity.

Ashe and Walker winced with every lash, their bodies jolting in the stunning pain. Several approaching Regulators, on discovering the mistreatment of these officers, shouted for them to stop.

"Taxed and robbed me into bankruptcy," yelled one. "And after I went to live with my folks, they got robbed out, too!"

"Our women have been assaulted and humiliated," added another, laying on lashes at an increasing rate.

"My young'uns were taken into service!" raged yet another, also quickening his strokes.

"What're ye doing, there! Give it up, men!" shouted Robert. "Stop it, now!" cried some. "No more of this!" echoed others.

Still another remarked, "If this be the game, I'll have naught to do with it!"

"Aye, yea, and amen," and "I'll quit and return home, if this be the plan," came the reply from others.

Ashe and Walker were untied and given back their coats, though their pistols and swords were confiscated. Robert and increasing numbers of men began to surround the two officers. Slowly but clearly Ashe and Walker seemed to reflect sympathy for the plight of these downtrodden colonials. Yet they remained silent.

"We—we had no idea. We're sorry for any injustices done to you!" Ashe finally mumbled. "But it wasn't us."

BLOOD AT ALAMANCE!

"I regret this unfortunate incident, Colonel," said Robert. "Hit's not our aim to abuse anybidy."

"And who might you be?" queried Ashe.

"Don't ye tell 'im, Cap'n Messer!" quipped one Regulator.

A laugh arose from the crowd. Robert smiled and shook his head as he continued, "Well, sir, now that hit's out. I am Captain Robert Messer. We are bound to ask the Governor to correct the atrocities being committed upon our good, honest people—devout subjects of the King."

One by one men unfolded their accounts of the terrible harassments and exploitations received under the heavy hand of Tryon and his cronies.

Robert, on sensing the officers' newly experienced remorse, allowed them to be kept under guard in the rear, with the stern directive that all reasonable courtesies were to be rendered them.

Word ran up and down the line that the Regulators were to rest in place and draw up further plans for the morrow, then camp on the present site for the night.

As the day wore on, Tryon fretted and paced in front of his tent. "Any word from Ashe?" he asked, worriedly.

"None, sir," replied Fanning. "Would it please Your Excellency if I mounted and reconnoitered?" he offered, with feigned and uncommitted words.

"Well, we know enough already. We know where the rebels will be camped. We march at daybreak!"

"May it be the last daybreak they ever see!" Fanning added with a cold grin, peering sideways to calculate the Governor General's reaction, ever hoping to curry favor and ingratiate himself.

Tryon turned and expressed puzzlement, then smiled.

Tryon's plan was to surprise the Regulators. He ordered his men to march in silence, without drums, leaving their camp standing under guard. Their approach up the Salisbury Road went undetected. On arriving in Alamance, he set up his line of battle within a half mile of the Regulators' camp.

He ordered his artillery to be set up in the center of the front line, facing a large open field. As they rolled and

TURNER

creaked into place, he positioned ranks of men on both sides of the cannon emplacements, then 100 yards behind he established a second rank of men. Fanning was placed in command of the front left, and Col. Richard Caswell the front right. The rear rank's wings were commanded by Cols. Leech and Thompson.

A rear guard was formed with Royal Militia infantry from Wake, and a lighthorse detachment from Duplin. Rangers served as outriders, keeping watch on the flanks, while Orange County's own lighthorse detachment served as Tryon's personal guard.

Company commanders were already reporting significant numbers of deserters; men who, on learning they were to attack their own kith and kin, elected to withdraw from the field.

"Oh, to have regular Royal troops!" Tryon bellowed, "Rather than colonials among my ranks!"

"Those who would desert are not worthy of Your Excellency's command. Better to be done with them. May they hang like the colonial dogs they are!" Fanning rejoined.

"Time, Edmund—and the momentum of events—will bring all to justice," Tryon replied in pauses and whispers, preoccupied with scouring the wood line with his spyglass. Every slight movement or shadow alerted him. He would swing his spyglass upward and lean quickly forward in his saddle, as though his eyes were going to pop through the instrument. Then he would sit back and lower it again.

The Regulators were awakened by the approach of Alexander Martin and Rev. David Caldwell on horseback, with shouts of "Hello, in the camp!" They had ridden with the Sheriff to Tryon's camp to urge him to hold off on doing battle, until attempts could be made at negotiations. Tryon had nodded his consent, though fighting blood still boiled in his veins. Sheriff Butler wisely remained behind in Tryon's camp, knowing he was the cause of much of their furor. Butler rode slowly over to Tryon, smiling in an attempt to ingratiate himself to him, the highest power in the colony. But Tryon turned aside, snubbing him. He then rode over

BLOOD AT ALAMANCE!

toward Fanning, who likewise snubbed him, turning away as he approached.

By now, many Regulators were convinced there would be no fight, and indeed wanted none. But the complaints of the awakening Regulators buzzed about these visitors' ears like a swarm of hornets. Seeing the Regulators had no intention of disbanding, the men made several trips back and forth between the two camps, urging restraint.

The leaders of the Regulators jointly drew up a petition to confer with the Governor, on the matter of settling their disputes. Alexander and Caldwell, on their last trip to the Regulator camp, agreed to take the petition to Tryon. On receiving it, Tryon fumed with rage, bellowing out the order, "Bring up my Aide-de-Camp!"

Capt. Donald Malcolm rode up and saluted, and took verbal orders from the Governor. He then rode over with a flag of truce and spoke to the Regulators.

"His Excellency, Governor-General Tryon, sends you these words: *'Inasmuch as I have made every possible effort to quiet your unseemly disturbances, I have nothing more to offer, but to demand your immediate submission. You must promise to pay your taxes as presently due, lay down your arms, and disperse. You shall receive no further warning.'*"

The Regulators began to grumble, until their ire reached a bonding power. Then one man shouted, "No! No! No to Bully Billy!" The words began to be repeated by others until arising in a chant that compelled him to leave.

Another petition sent the evening before was only now being answered by Tryon, who had dictated his response into written form. The Regulator line was so stretched out and unorganized, a number of petitions had been sent to Tryon by various means, not all of them reaching him.

As his last act of communication Tryon dispatched another aide-de-camp, Capt. Philmore Hawkins, with the directive to read his document to the Regulators. On arrival at the Regulator camp, Hawkins remained in his saddle while reading the text aloud:

"*Alamance Camp, Thursday, May 16th, 1771. To Those Who Style Themselves "Regulators": In reply to your petition*

TURNER

of yesterday, I am to acquaint you that I have ever been attentive to the interests of your County and to every individual residing therein. I lament the fatal necessity to which you have now reduced me by withdrawing yourselves from the mercy of the Crown and from the laws of your country. I require you who are now assembled as Regulators to quietly lay down your arms, to surrender up your leaders, honour the laws of your country and rest on the leniency of the Government. By accepting these terms within one hour from the delivery of this dispatch, you will prevent an effusion of blood, as you are at this time in a state of REBELLION against your King, your country, and your laws. (Signed) William Tryon."

"Witness seal and coat of arms," added Hawkins, as he held the document up to their view. "And now, what say ye?" Hawkin's proclamation was met with less hostility than Malcolm's had been, many Regulators even appearing indifferent to the repetitive scene, and Tryon's empty words. Some of the younger among them had taken to wrestling and pine-cone fights, and other distractions. Soon men were taking out knives for whittling or playing mumbly-peg, while others began to deal cards.

But shortly after Hawkins had withdrawn, the shout of military orders were being heard, as Tryon's men advanced their position closer to theirs. Regulators began to regain their feet, and to retrieve their muskets.

CHAPTER SEVEN

H**ERMAN** Husband plodded along through the woods on his horse, humming hymns and uttering occasional prayers for his fellow Regulators as they faced the apex of their life of tribulations. He had done all within his power to secure for them the basic rights of humanity, even being jailed for it, and falsely accused. And now this gentle man of peace, and good neighbor to many, was being hunted like a detested beast.

Born into wealthy circumstances in Maryland, he was raised on good manners, honest labor, and fair treatment of fellowman. His native intelligence, and keen eye for grace and sophistication, had led him to be viewed as a gentleman of higher standing than his otherwise modest appearance would suggest. Ever searching for spiritual meaning in his life, he was drawn to the Quaker community now growing in Maryland from nearby Pennsylvania. Their principles of modesty, fairness, mercy, industrious self-motivation, and peace appealed strongly to his inner nature. Forsaking the Anglican Church, he found a haven for his soul amongst the Quakers.

Over time his fellow Quakers began to look upon him skeptically as he matured, developing an irrepressible interest in society and sophistication beyond farm life. His reading of scholarly works worried some folk, though he balanced this with daily devotion to Scripture study.

Even his demeanor did not fit the mold. Although his Quaker folk were of a positive and bright spirit, he beamed and smiled and laughed aloud far more than one would typically encounter within his socio-religious milieu. His plump cheeks and stout belly would jiggle in harmony with his hearty bursts of laughter, often going so far as to chortle. But shocking as his mirth may have been, his purity

TURNER

and obvious love for all people earned him a considerable degree of acceptance within a society of quasi-austerity.

Stout he was, but in a bullish sort of strength; not as a plump or fleshy being. He could outlift, outthrow, and outrun his peers, but would always apologize humbly for any showiness on his part. The modest girls of his village always diverted their eyes when he looked their way, as if to hide the fact that they found him handsome. Broad and round in the shoulder, full at the neck, and with a large and well-formed head, he carried himself well; and no matter how humbly he tried to comport himself, he always gathered admiring glances wherever he went.

His regulation beard, covering the jaws and chin only, he kept neatly trimmed as compared to his comrades, maintaining just enough outgrowth to satisfy what was expected of a Quaker lad as he reached young manhood. Likewise his thick black hair he wore just long enough to reach his collar, but never enough to tie back at the nape. His clothes he kept neat at all times, even if having to change in the middle of a work day. Still he was not vain in respect to outward pretense; he rather leaned toward a tidy appearance as an outward sign of inner orderliness.

His unquenchable thirst for learning beyond the fundamentals led him to books and social interactions alien to his peers. He always spoke inquisitively to outsiders who stopped at any shop or house near his, in quest of goods to buy. Often this led to intense conversations and explorations of the world beyond his narrow domain. Others of his community would listen intently at first, then begin to drift several feet away as if in fear of the forbidden. Still, some would linger afar off and continue to observe this rarity among them as he gleaned knowledge and culture.

He also learned to make money as a natural matter of course; first by maximizing production of salable farm goods and livestock, then handcrafted harness and saddlery, and eventually taking clerical work in village businesses which led to being entrusted with management

BLOOD AT ALAMANCE!

tasks. In time he had made himself independently wealthy with farming, land speculation, and copper mining.

Seeking to advance himself in town life, amidst the cares of the world, brought such a degree of scrutiny upon him that he felt it best to move on before being called to discipline by the elders. As many Quakers began to migrate south into North Carolina, he found ample opportunity to invest in good land, where with industry and wise investment of means and time, he developed a fine plantation of 10,000 acres at Sandy Creek, near Hillsborough. While he followed his own natural path according to the dictates of his sense of enlightenment, he never drifted from the values and good conscience he had gained from his upbringing. His sense of social duty, willingness to sacrifice for others, and steady reliability brought him continued success among fellow colonists. All in all, he was a well rounded man and an asset to his community, which led to his eventual election to the Assembly.

Though he did not state so openly, even down in North Carolina his own church suggested excommunicating him for involvement in worldly matters, including government with all its scandal and squabble. As an Assemblyman and social reformer, he had to play as tough as his pacifist beliefs would allow him, ever presenting an air of peace and forbearance while standing for principle; yet even these acts were considered too conformed to the world to satisfy his church elders. Thus he sacrificed his standing within both extremes of society: the taunting and the tame. And now, tugging at his heart was the likelihood that he would have to abandon his beloved plantation at Sandy Creek.

Today many new worries, burdens heretofore alien to him, weighted down his shoulders—but not his heart. Every time he entered a road, he would soon after have to dart back into the woods at the sound of approaching hoof beats. Observing sheepishly from the concealment of tree and bush, he would often see soldiers scurrying to and fro, as if bent on some vital errand.

TURNER

He resumed his woodland journey for a time. Then approaching a cleared field he observed a poor old farmer at his plow, drawn by an even poorer-and-older-looking horse. He hailed this tiller of the soil with the greeting, "Heaven bless thee, neighbor!"

The old man reined up with a startled "Whoa!", then skeptically nodded at Herman.

"I'm interested in a horse trade, sir," Herman said.

"Sha, ye say ye are?" replied the old man.

"Amen, brother, that I am." Herman patted the neck of his obviously superior horse, and added, "I'm rather pressed for business. What dost thou think of swapping this mount, for yours?"

"Uh—ye mean, *this'un hyar?*" The man wiped his wet brow with his tattered sleeve, his mouth agape with astonishment.

"Well, she be a saddle horse. Thou mayest need to break her to the plow. But she be gentle as a butterfly and minds what she's told." The man stood stupefied while Herman began to unharness the plow horse. "I reckon it's agreed then?"

"Ye're a Quaker, air ye?"

"Society of Friends, by birth and heritage. What think thee of an even trade, horse for horse?"

"Why, I reckon hit's a deal, all right!" The man trembled with unbelief as he began to excitedly assist Herman with removing the harness from his old fleabag critter.

"I'll keep my saddle, though. But to make it even, I'll swap coats and hats with thee!" Herman tossed an eye toward the man's old coat, hanging on the snake-rail fence.

The man nodded, still overwhelmed, until finally replying, "Uh—sure thang! I'll fetch hit fer ye."

As Herman placed his saddle on the nigh-swayed back of the old horse, the farmer gathered his wits sufficiently to say, "But I have no bill of sale!"

"I'll write one out for thee, directly." Herman removed a writing kit from his saddle bag, and scratched out a brief document for the man which read, *"For value received, one aged gray plowhorse in trade, I hereby transfer to—*

BLOOD AT ALAMANCE!

(What name sir?—Hezekiah Yearwood)—*my sorrel mare, 14 hands high, 6 year of age, with flaxen mane and tail and a white sock on her left rear leg. Witness my signature this 16th day of May, year of our Lord 1771...*"

Herman handed the unsigned document to the old man, who queried, "And what be yer name, sir?"

"Uh—well..." replied Herman, as he tugged on the old coat. He stalled for time as he mounted the nag. "I'm thinking it over."

"Ye got a name, don't'chee? I cain't read, but I kin tell whur a name's s'pose to be, at the bottom!"

"Aye, that I do. But I'm not so certain it be a name thou needst be associating with at present."

"Uh—the mare—she's yorn to trade, fair an' clear, ain't she?"

Realizing it may be days before any literate person might happen to see the mare and suspect the farmer's sudden good fortune, moreover to ask to see the bill of sale with it's tell-tale signature, Herman pulled out his quill kit again, took the paper, and signed it.

"There, now, good neighbor. The mare was mine, free and clear. And now she be thine. But thou needst not be informing folks about me for at least two, three days. Least wise, not what I look like!" With that, he placed his nice new hat on the farmer's head.

The farmer gently shook his head in disbelief, his mouth still drooping in bewilderment. Herman waved the farmer's old hat in the air, plopped it on his head, and sallied toward the Virginia Road. His spirits were elevated now that his disguise allowed him to travel on the public thoroughfare, leisurely and without fear of capture.

He passed the time humming hymns again, and occasionally chuckling at his own absurdity. Within an hour he came to a river ferry being guarded by three Redcoats. To further conceal his identity, he began to sing.

But he didn't merely sing. He sang loudly, off key, and made up rambling hymn-like words to a made up tune:

"Repent—all ye lands!
The day—be nigh at hand!
An accounting ye must give, of every day ye live;

TURNER

So repent ye, while ye cannnnnn!"

"Halt! Who goes there!" shouted a corporal, as the guards all wheeled about to witness this unexpected scene. "Advance and be recognized!"

"Halt! Halt, indeed! That is the word from Above, dear brethren! Halt from the erroneous ways of this wicked world!"

"Oh, just a crazy old preacher," the corporal said, as his comrades chuckled amongst themselves. "Where'ye bound?"

"Oh, I be bound to yon fair village, and beyond, wher'er my calling—and my stalwart stallion—may lead, my son! I be a-sowing the Word!" Then leaning over in the corporal's face, he wheezed, "Dost thou need repenting, lad? Hast thou time to hear the word? I've a sermon hereabout somewhere." Herman fumbled about in his coat pockets. "I'll preach it unto thee!"

"Well, that sure ain't the Herman Husband we're to look for," one soldier said to the other. "He's a gentleman, atop a fine steed."

"And a man of learning. Er—beggin' yer pardon, yer holiness," scoffed another soldier, tipping his hat in mock courtesy.

"I have it here, someplace," Herman continued. "Wouldst I shall preach it unto thee? I shall, presently."

"Er—that can wait for another time, elder brother," the corporal remarked. "But ye can take a message for me across the river, to the Squire of the next village." He wrote out a note and handed it to Herman.

"Here, now, old reverend," the corporal continued. "If ye'll carry this on to the Squire, ye may pass."

"Amen, brethren," Herman said, suppressing an emerging grin. "Sure thou hast no time for a sermon? Thou never knowest when..."

"Get along, now! That message is of vital importance!"

Herman nodded, waved farewell to the guards, and rode slowly on his way, wailing out his homespun hymn. After ferrying across the river, he took the note from his pocket and read with sudden mirth: *"Beware of one Herman Husband escaping by this road, genteel*

BLOOD AT ALAMANCE!

appearance and fine sorrel mare. Wanted by Gov. Tryon for high treason."

With a chuckle in his heart and a smile upon his countenance, Herman rode directly to the Squire of the town, and presented the message as directed. The Squire became animated with excitement, and was most appreciative. He then wrote out a pass for him to journey on his way, which said: *"Allow the bearer to travel at will. He is a man of great integrity and loyalty to the Crown, and has rendered much aide in our effort to trap the outlaw Herman Husband."*

Herman rode peacefully and at his own leisurely pace, bound for his native Pennsylvania. He was never aware of the military standoff that sat poised for potential battle and bloodshed back in Alamance, though he was being blamed as its cause.

Back at the Messer farm, the womenfolk of their settlement were abuzz with news and gossip coming down the roads. There were many speculative accounts of what was taking place, but a central theme seemed to weave through every new tale: The Regulators had stood to arms, and were marching on Tryon's camp in Alamance.

Mary's neighbor, Becky Nix, dusted up the road in a near-trot as she scurried to the Messer cabin.

"Mary! Mary!" she called out from the yard. Mary and her children spilled out the door with astonished faces. "Mary, have ye heered? They've marched to petition Tryon. But he's brought his army out to Alamance!"

"Is there—fighting?" Mary asked with quivering lips.

"No word as yet. But our menfolk have camped too, and hit looks mighty like they's fixin' to have at it!"

Christian and Tipton shouted "Hoorah!", and began to play like soldiers firing muskets. Without another thought Mary whirled about and said, "Mary-Ann, fetch me a tow sack and that half-cake of cornbread. Joseph, fetch the butcher knife."

"You going to battle, too, Maw?" asked Joseph. "Not much of a sword," added Tipton.

Mary took the knife to the smoke house and cut off a big portion of cured ham, and dropped it into the cloth

TURNER

sack with the cornbread. She arranged for Becky to mind the young'uns as she and Christian headed on foot for Alamance.

BLOOD AT ALAMANCE!

CHAPTER EIGHT

FAR from Herman Husband, the troubled waters of Alamance began to emit vapors of steam, nearing the boiling point. Neither side showed any hint of backing down. Tryon's camp assumed offensive posture now. The Regulators' long thin line tensed and released, like the muscles of a man contemplating possible assault. A newborn battle was in its initial birth pains.

By May 15, Tryon had bivouacked his troops on the plantation of Capt. Michael Holt. He received a message from the Regulators under a flag of truce, demanding a review of injustices done them, proposing certain steps for redress, and an answer to be sent forth within four hours. Tryon promised an answer by noon on the morrow.

The men known as Regulators were of a rugged constitution, formulated from oppression and knit together by integrity. Men of concern had now become men of commitment. Countless numbers from Orange and surrounding counties had already risked life and property by signing Regulation petitions to the Governor. There was no turning back. Now, these men of commitment would have to stand as men of courage. Their very survival depended on it.

Courageous men were now catapulted into the role of leading these fellow countrymen. Some were local militia officers, ministers, or respected community figures. Chief among these were Capt. Benjamin Merrill of the Rowan County Militia, and Capt. Robert Messer of Orange County. Jim Hunter, dubbed the "General of the Regulators" for his daring overall leadership in months past, was now in hiding from Tryon's rage. With scattered company-level military leadership, the Regulators were essentially a combination of moderately trained militia members combined with an untrained swarm of hornets, a hodgepodge with little overriding tactical military cohesiveness, and indeed very little ammunition on hand.

Absent a central military head or organized leadership structure, these respected principals could do little more than send words of encouragement up and down the line: First priority, seek a peaceful resolution. Second priority, stand firm for the cause, with nary a man backing down. Robert continued to subtly check his musket and ammunition, and to seek any updated intelligence, careful not to elicit alarm by his actions which might intimate that impending action was foremost in his mind.

But the scent of battle was in the air, and he could no longer pretend it away. Careful not to excite tension, Robert sat and calmly conferred a moment with a half dozen leaders of the Movement. He drew lines on the ground with a stick, pointing at various positions and indicating possible movements.

"Not to suggest anything adverse is going to happen. But just imagining that it does…"

"Hit's alright, Captain Messer," Tyson Noblet interrupted, a militia leftenant from Rowan County. "We're prepared to face whatever comes."

"They will begin with cannon fire," Robert noted. "If we can place heavy fire upon the artillery—if they be within our musket range—we will be the better suited for surviving the first volleys."

"Shall we charge them, Captain? For once they suffer the loss of cannon, I doubt the others will advance."

"No, we can fight a defensive battle from the edge of the woods. They will be more likely to charge on us, especially horsemen. Fire on them first, if they come at us." After a momentary pause, Robert looked toward Noblet again and added, "But if the cannon fire proves too much, we can rush the guns and overtake them."

Then an old Scotsman named Patrick Muller, a veteran of the Royal Army, spoke up. "Aye, and if they charge, they will have the advantage of bayonet and sword," he explained from obvious experience. His leathery face was lined with wrinkles, as if the lines of war maps had weathered into his skin. He spoke with a confidence that

BLOOD AT ALAMANCE!

comes from a lifetime of experience, or several lifetimes within one. Through the croaky, lyrical accent resounded a tone of sharp, here-and-now reality, a result of years in battle and facing death up close and personally.

"Go on, sir," Robert quietly urged.

"Then, our only chance will be to encircle them before our ball and powder be spent, cutting off both flanks. This we do by remaining spread out in a long line, as we are, until we close around them like great wings. Notice they be fairly trapped in yonder roadway now, and with little room to move to one side or t'other."

"That appears to be our best chance."

"I say *only* chance, Captain, for the chance of retreat is not open to us, for they will run us down. But it do be, to them. If they see us encircling them, they may retreat to their rear. But even better, if we do surround and overpower them, we will have our choice of terms. Either way, we have victory." His matter-of-fact observations shocked the men around him into a clearer focus on impending reality, yet seemed to generate a sense of safety under the wise strength of his tutelage.

Robert and the others nodded in agreement. Thankful to have a salty veteran in their ranks, Robert patted him on the back as he arose and returned to his own men.

Passing by so many dedicated fellowmen, he shared nods of understanding and silent mutual commitment. But he would encounter occasional voices bemoaning their status with questions such as, "Tryon's got a trained army, Captain. What have we got?", or, "They are skilled troops, sir. What are our skills?"

Robert would straighten his back, hold high his chin, and reply, "We have courage—marksmanship—and the cause of right! We fight for our very families and farms. What have they to fight for? A bully tyrant!"

Men would cheer at hearing these words. There was no question about their courage and cause. But they were proud, too, of their keen marksmanship. Frontiersmen generally were, and welcomed any opportunity to demonstrate same.

TURNER

Robert and the other leaders spoke with their men up and down the line about possible battle plans, in the event the present pressures did not culminate in squeezing some civil reasoning from Tryon's bullish head. Several men began pointing in various directions, then squatting on the ground to draw in the dirt with a twig, as a number of potential strategies were put forth.

An old gentleman named Thompson had earlier volunteered to cross into Tryon's camp under a flag of truce to negotiate terms. He took with him Robert Matear, a complete neutral who had never joined the Regulator Movement. Hours later, they had not returned. Tensions mounted throughout the morning. About noon, the Regulators began to step out of the wood line and onto the edge of the meadow. Tryon's men had advanced their line to within about 100 yards of the Regulators. Rev. Caldwell rode forward again to make one last plea against bloodshed.

"Gentlemen and Regulators!" he called out from his saddle. "Those of you who are not too far committed should desist and quietly return to your homes. Those of you who have lain yourselves liable should submit without resistance. I and others promise to obtain for you the best possible terms. The Governor will grant you nothing. You are unprepared for war! You have no cannon! You have no substantial or cohesive military training! You have no commanding officers to lead you in battle. You have no ammunition. You shall be defeated, and for naught!"

Common grumbling ran up and down the line. Old Muller yelled back toward Caldwell with his Scottish brogue and air of command, "Ye'd best be moving on, Reverend, for Tryon's men'll shoot ye in the back! Aye, parley be over, and Tryon has no more love for ye than for us!"

One Regulator shouted angrily: "We will not lie down and be trampled by Tryon!" He was followed by hundreds of equally enraged voices, crying, "No! No! No to Bully Billy!", fueled by a fury that could have been defused by Tryon's simply discussing the issues so obviously destroying the colony.

BLOOD AT ALAMANCE!

Tryon's forces advanced steadily, from 100 yards' distance, to 50 yards, like a sea of red intent on flowing over them, their drums and fifes filling the air with pomp. The advance halted at a mere 25 yards from the Regulators, yet they gave no sign of being intimidated.

Regulators began to chant, "Go ahead and fire, Tryon!" and "Fire on me!" Men ran forward from the trees, bearing their chests and shouting defiantly, "Fire on me!"

Tryon was holding Thompson and Matear as prisoners. The time for talking was clearly over. Thompson was an outspoken gentleman of the highest character, whose only act had been to broker peace. Yet Tryon would not let him go. Thompson stood erect and boldly exclaimed, "Now Governor, you know my mission is ended. I came with Matear under no obligation to either camp. We have business elsewhere, and will now take leave of you."

"Halt where you are, Thompson!" bellowed Tryon, like a raging bull. Matear stood aloof and observant.

"Governor, I am a nonpartisan gentleman. I am unarmed. I am taking leave of you now. Surely you will not shoot an innocent old man in the back." Thompson stood erect and squared his aged shoulders. There was distinction in his intelligent voice, though a noble sort of humility was immediately evident as he spoke. He stood as a genuine model of peace and goodwill, calm and assured in the midst of pending chaos. The certainty of his character presented a poetic irony in the face of abject uncertainty, even seeming to assuage the tense mood of several of the soldiers near him.

With this, Thompson began to casually walk away along the left flank, toward neutral ground. Tryon reached over from his horse and grabbed a musket from a soldier, and—Thompson's confidence notwithstanding—shot him squarely in the back, killing him instantly.

Tryon then threw down the musket, exclaiming, "Oh Heavens, what have I done!" Realizing the gross error of his hotheaded deed, he turned to Fanning and commanded, "Quickly, send forth a man under a flag of truce. Perhaps they did not see whom I shot! Or, at least, we may forestall their revenge!" Matear remained under guard.

TURNER

Fanning dispatched the Governor's aide Donald Malcolm again, but many Regulators had indeed seen Tryon's act of murder, and began firing at Malcolm; but mercifully just in front of his feet. He beat a hasty retreat to the safety of his own lines, stumbling as his breeches fell.

Tryon screamed like a beast, "How dare they fire on my flag of truce!" Already he had forgotten about Thompson and his own banner of amity. He stood high in his stirrups and shouted, "Fire!" Yet no one fired.

He began to race his white charger up and down the ranks, shouting at the infantry and artillery, "Fire!" Still there was no response. His own troops hadn't the heart nor will to fire on these innocent men, particularly after witnessing the murder of poor old Thompson.

"Fire, I say!" Tryon ranted. He became maniacal as he raced his horse in circles now, screaming, "Fire on them, or fire on me!"

A Regulator shouted back, "Fire and be doomed!" His warning was suddenly echoing like thunder among the Regulators: "Fire and be doomed!"

Like dueling volcanoes, musket fire erupted swiftly and fiercely from both sides. The air filled with a swarm of the militiamen's high-caliber projectiles, answered defiantly by the Regulators' whining homemade bullets.

As if following a mass instinct, the Regulators fell back behind the trees and rocks and continued to fill the air with scores of well-placed rounds, felling many of the Governor's men who were hard pressed to return fire as rapidly, whether with musketry or cannon, due to their position of exposure and no opportunity for cover.

As a few of Tryon's men momentarily improved in their musket fire, Robert shouted over his shoulder, "Call for Pugh!" The order echoed all along the Regulator line, "Call for Pugh!" James Pugh, one of the most outstanding marksmen in the colony, ran forth and knelt by Robert's side. Robert patted his shoulder and asked, "How can we best put your shooting to advantage, James?"

"I'll get atop that big rock," answered Pugh. "And take three men to stand behind me and reload."

BLOOD AT ALAMANCE!

Soon Pugh was safely concealed and firing expertly, dispatching instant death from an excellent vantage point. Exchanging each emptied musket with the men behind him for a freshly loaded one, he was able to keep up a deadly stream of fire that baffled and frightened the enemy, confusing their efforts and scattering them.

The front infantry ranks fell far back, retreating past the artillery pieces which had stood farther down range from them, leaving the gunnerymen to stand alone in the field.

The artillery colonel ordered his commanders to aim pistols at their hesitant gunners, then shouted, "Fire now, or we will shoot you down like treasonous dogs!" The Governor's artillery fired a volley, which flew well over the Regulators. Their colonel screamed, "Aim lower!" The next volley also went well above the Regulators' heads. It appeared there was widespread reluctance among their ranks to fire upon the Regulators, which infuriated Tryon all the more.

"Direct your fire to the artillery," shouted Robert. The tactic worked swiftly as a hail of bullets showered down upon the gun emplacements, with the few surviving artillerymen falling back in retreat.

"Stand your ground," shouted several of their officers. "Regroup, and prepare to charge!" But the Redcoats and yellow-cockaded militiamen did not advance.

Capt. Montgomery of Surry County seized the moment and ordered a charge of his company of Regulators. They drove the remaining militia completely from the field, who left two of their cannons behind.

Two spirited young lads, the MacPherson brothers, ran forth from the woods and seized a cannon, turning it toward Tryon's disjointed swarm of men. Then realizing they lacked the knowledge to fire it, they ran back to their own lines with the field piece in tow. Several boys laughed and cheered, slapping the big gun and sitting astride it, playing with it almost as if it were a big toy.

All but routed, the Governor's forces did get off another few rounds of artillery from a greater distance, one shell killing Capt. Montgomery. But the Governor's Militia

TURNER

remained in disarray. Tryon was in an utter state of exasperation.

Fanning, in a show of ineptitude and cowardice, fell back with his entire regiment. Regulators swarmed forth boldly onto the field, taking advantage of the chance to keep their opponents at bay with flying lead. It was a field day for frontier marksmen, who were trained by hunting for food to make every shot count.

Fanning whirled about on his horse in panic, mumbling to himself, "What shall we do? What *shall* we *do?*" Then on eyeing Tryon riding toward him, he nervously waved his sword in the air, feigning bravado, and shouted, "Rally, men! Forward!", though no men were near him. But as Tryon received a bullet through his hat, he turned and rode away from Fanning, seeking to save himself from death or capture, either of which fate would lead to ultimate humiliation.

"Steady fire, men! But clearly aimed!" shouted Robert, as he methodically fired, reloaded, and fired again, each time felling a foe.

Realizing the need to buy more time and save his own imperial hide, Tryon rode back over to Fanning and shouted, "Your sword, Edmund!" Bewildered, Fanning began to hand it over to his commander. "No, tie this to it." Tryon handed him a white scarf. "Ride out with another flag of truce! It is our only option, presently!"

Seeing Tryon whirl about to duck bullets whizzing past him, Fanning quickly tossed the scarf to a mounted ranger and said, "Here, go forth with this flag of truce! General Tryon's orders! Tell them we seek to talk terms!"

The ranger rode forth with blind obedience, the scarf streaming from his sword. Several Regulators yelled, "Flag of truce! Hold your fire!" But others saw only a charging solder with a drawn saber, and suspecting an enemy advance, instantly cut him down with withering musket fire.

Tryon, seeing the man fall, spun about on his horse and yelled at his forces, "The rebels have shot down our flag of truce! This means certain death, without mercy, for both you and me! Officers, organize for a charge!"

BLOOD AT ALAMANCE!

But his leaders, like his men, were too scattered and pinned down to mount a charge. Tryon remained behind the relative safety of his men, peering through his spyglass. Potshots were exchanged between Royal Militia and Regulators for the better part of an hour. Many of Tryon's men deserted, while most lay quivering on the ground or crouched behind the cannons. Any attempt by Tryon's troops to maneuver to either flank was hemmed back in by musket fire of deadly accuracy, usually coming from places of concealment. Occasionally one of the disrupted gun crews tried futilely to get off another round of artillery, driven away from their big guns every time by musket fire.

At length the Regulators' gunfire began to subside. Tryon put on a face of renewed courage and announced, "See, men! The rebels' ammunition is running out! We shall charge upon my command! Reorganize the artillery, and resume firing!"

Colonels, majors, captains, leftenants, and sergeants rattled off orders and threats like a herd of fierce lions. "Rally, men!"—"Fix bayonets!"—"All charge, or die!"

"Every man of you is accounted for, and those who do not charge will be shot for treason this day!" shouted Tryon. Waving sabers high, his officers echoed his command, *"Forward!"* Having been routed by the Regulators, only half of whom actually fought and who only withdrew after their ammunition was expended, Tryon seized the opportunity to claim a hollow victory.

Following a few rounds of artillery fire, some of which found true their mark and felled several Regulators, men and horses began to surge up the meadow again. Pugh's helpers fell back in the face of overwhelming forces. Seeing his plight and the certainty of his capture, he elected to remain atop his perch and defend the men's escape, firing and reloading for himself, dropping Tryon's men until he was physically overtaken.

Fanning, remaining safely in the rear, spied James Few walking along beyond the right flank, merely a detached observer of the tumultuous events.

TURNER

"Ho, there! Few!" shouted Fanning. But Few did not respond. Fanning spurred his horse toward him and reined up, cutting off his path. "I say, Few! What are you about?"

Few looked slowly upward at Fanning, lackadaisical in his demeanor, as if unaffected by anything around him. "Few, give an accounting for yourself!" Fanning demanded. But James only mumbled a few incoherent syllables. "Why, you've lost your mind, Few! Barmy as a loon!" And rightfully so, inasmuch as Fanning's breaking him financially and emotionally, then violently taking his beloved Cordelia from him, had indeed driven him quite mad from the hopelessness imposed upon him.

"You men, come over here!" Fanning called to four cowering stragglers. "And bring a rope. You will be given the opportunity to redeem your cowardice, by executing an enemy of the Crown!" He then whispered to James, "Your darling Cordelia need no longer be encumbered by any promise to you, madman! She'll now begin to feel freer than my methods of discipline have thus far rendered her!"

Turning about in his saddle, Fanning called out to the stragglers again, "Well, what shall it be, men? Execute my order, or find yourselves executed this very hour!"

The young men ran half-heartedly toward James, who became startled now, and stumbled backward behind some trees. "Seize him, ye laggards!" Fanning snarled, practically frothing.

A couple of the men pretended to be grabbing James behind the trees. Seeing he was indeed a madman, as Fanning had declared—albeit an innocent madman—one of the soldiers whispered to him, "Run for it, man!"

James seemed even more confused, so the men pushed him onward, one nudging him with his bayonet. He seemed to comprehend the need to flee at last. One of the men yelled backward over his shoulder for the benefit of Fanning's ears, "Halt! Or we fire!" Then elbowing a comrade and signaling with a wink, they both fired high over James' head as he disappeared into the woods.

"Contemptible cur! You'll have to reckon with me yet, Few!" Fanning shouted toward the woods. "Well, then,

BLOOD AT ALAMANCE!

onward, you men! Follow me!" He spurred his steed forward to catch up with Tryon.

As Tryon's men advanced toward the woods and passed their original line along the roadway, they soon surrounded and captured fifteen Regulators: those slightly wounded, and those assisting them from the field. Among them were several leaders. He ordered his men to surround the woods into which most Regulators had taken refuge. "Set the woods afire!" he ordered.

Suddenly some unseen Regulators fired from concealment up in the trees, dropping Redcoats and militiamen like flies. Tryon's rallying forces stopped in their tracks, and fell back several yards. The firing slowly subsided as the Regulators withdrew from the woods.

"General," remarked Solomon Woody, a captive held under guard. "Our men have fled beyond these woods. Only our wounded lie there now!"

"Then, let them burn in their stead! Light the forest!"

CHAPTER NINE

TRYON'S foot soldiers balked at carrying out his hideous order to burn the wounded Regulators alive where they lay. Some sat down, confused and exhausted.

"Get to your feet, you spineless cowards!" bellowed Tryon. "You have seen the King's justice carried out this day. Stand courageous! Or be marked as traitors!"

"Yes, men! Stand courageous!" echoed the snake Fanning, as he rode up from his evil doing. "Honor, above all!"

"Colonel Fanning!" snapped Tryon, stunned to see him alive. "I saw you fall as you rode forth bearing a flag of truce!"

Fanning hung his head in mock mourning and replied, "As I endeavored to do so, sir, a remarkably brave ranger grabbed my saber from me, and spurred his mount nobly up the hill where he fell! A true credit to King and country!"

"Men, here is our brave Colonel Fanning, back from the clutches of death! Follow his example, buck up, and carry out my order!"

Men reluctantly began to set the woods afire. Dryness and a steady breeze soon fanned the flames into an inferno. Moans of the wounded Regulators had already filled the air with an uneasy chill. But by the time the flames engulfed them, moans turned to screams of agony which the Royalists found unbearable. Some wept; others fell sick.

Fanning cracked his mouth as if to utter words of chastisement to them, then on seeing Tryon apparently about to engage in the same, held his tongue. He observed Tryon closely, ever vigilant for any opportunity to be ingratiating. But Tryon, too, restrained his words as he and Fanning turned to ride away, as if to hide from their

BLOOD AT ALAMANCE!

men the sickened expressions now sweeping over their own faces.

They found a distraction by riding over to inspect the captured Regulators. Tryon was already working out the details of his official report in his mind, lying aloud to his officers about killing several score of the Regulators and losing but nine of his own men. They who rode along with him cast astonished eyes at each other, astounded at his boastful horn-blowing, knowing full well that several of their units were decimated.

On seeing so many of his own men lying wounded and being carried from the field, Tryon said in an aside to two of his lesser staff officers, "Remove our wounded to Captain Holt's house, yonder. Establish a hospital there. I shall inspect same, presently." He then resumed prattling to his note-taking aides about his distorted post-battle calculations. "With the fervor so characteristic of our King's own troops, these gallant men—led by officers so capable and true—charged the rebels without regard for life or limb, conquering with every step until all opposition was destroyed, devastated, or dispersed..."

Naturally, casualty figures varied widely between the two camps. But the Regulators truthfully estimated nine of their 2,000 were dead on the field of battle, though with a great number wounded; but then a great many of these were burned to death afterward as they lay helpless. They estimated seventy Royalists were killed.

Yet the Royalists' wounded were difficult for the Regulators to calculate, since they set about carrying them from the field before the gun smoke had fully cleared the air. They hastened to remove their dead as well, under orders to minimize the visual evidence of their losses. But every Regulator who fought knew full well that scores of Tryon's unfortunate men were put out of action.

Fanning rounded up his subordinate officers and began to give after-action directives: "Organize details to gather all fallen arms and ordnance, friendly and enemy. Search the countryside for deserters, and bind them over for court-martial. Inspect every soldier's weapon to determine if any have not been fired today. Any man suspected of failing to have fired a single round, will be tried for insubordination and cowardice in the face of the enemy! Cowardice and dishonor shall not be tolerated one whit, in service to His Majesty!"

Tryon looked over the prisoners for several pulsating minutes, riding slowly around them, frequently opening his mouth to make a comment; then shutting it again as if in contemplation of the oddity of the scene. Though he would not admit it, these common men managed the wherewithal to rout his forces and place his life and career in grave peril. He continued to study them as though they were museum pieces from his life's history, strangers standing as determinants of his own fate, humble individuals comprising a united whole bent on altering the course of his life and the future of the British Empire.

Fanning rode slowly back to within Tryon's hearing, and summoned a scribe to take his dictation: "Dispatch this notice to New Bern, for circulation throughout the colony: *'An exemplary victory has been won with the defeat of the stubborn and imprudent rebels at Alamance, under the gallant leadership of our noble and victorious General Tryon, Governor of His Majesty's Province of North Carolina—Whom all revere . . .'* "

Fanning kept his eyes trained on Tryon while dictating, observing whether he was hearing his devious flattery. But Tryon, so deep in thought, seemed not to notice Fanning's glowing words of adulation.

At length Tryon uttered the order, "Search the prisoners—for weapons, notes, maps, anything that may reveal their vile purpose, and to be entered as evidence against them. Anything else of value, divide you amongst yourselves, you guards here present." Turning to the officers nearest him he explained, "Awarding the rebels' goods to these guards will more readily align them with a sense of loyalty to us, rather than the rabble under their watch!" Apparently Tryon was becoming keenly aware of the sympathies many of his own men held for his enemies, though none of those subservient to him would dare suggest so.

BLOOD AT ALAMANCE!

Mary and Christian Messer had walked rapidly for over six miles in quest of Robert, their bodies weary, but their spirits driving them onward. The holes, rocks and wagon wheel ruts were a continual annoyance to their feet and ankles, and more than once Mary faltered and Christian fell due to the uneven surface. Anxiety swelled in Mary's heart to see the roadways now filling with men and horses withdrawing from Alamance. After several passed by her, Mary asked some of them, "What has happened? Has there been trouble?"

Without stopping, men randomly answered her, "They's sure been a fight"—"Thar was a shootin' match, twixt us and them"—"The Regulators nigh defeated Tryon's army!"

"Then, why are ye leaving? Are there many of our menfolk hurt?" To these questions came no response.

"Have any of ye seen or heard ary a thing about Captain Messer? Robert Messer?" Mary would frequently call out to the men, and each time be answered with a shake of the head, or the simple but daunting apologies of "No, ma'am."

As the flow of men thinned to a trickle, she began to inquire of every man they encountered, "What of Captain Messer? Any word?"

Young Christian clung to his mother's trembling hand, seeking comfort from one who greatly needed comforting. Their hearts wove together in their shared anxiety, standing by the road, watching with the same thoughts and emotions, but sharing none by word. Christian was tall for his ten years, lean and wiry, and his complexion ruddy from a boy's life of working and romping in the summer sun. He pushed his brown hair from his eyes with his free hand, and Mary, suspecting he was wiping tears as well, lent a hand to assist with the task.

She released his hand and put her arm around his shoulder, as he put his around her waist. His physical tension eased somewhat now, as the virile young man drew strength from the strong tenderness of a brave and caring woman. Mary watched as another cluster of men came walking up the road, and resumed her inquiry, "Any word of Captain Messer? Robert Messer?"

TURNER

At length a solemn young man stopped and replied, "Ah, Captain Messer?" His grim demeanor softened to a smile. "Why, yes ma'am, what a grand fellow!"

"Then ye've seen him?" The words creaked from Mary's strained throat like spoken sobs.

Christian came from behind his mother's skirts to add, "Paw? Has he seen my paw?"

"Last I seen of 'im, he was a-leadin' men—brave men—and doin' an upmarket job of 'er!"

"But where is he now? Have ye seen any more of him?"

He shook his head sorrowfully and replied, "Sorry, ma'am, no. I reckon I've not. But ye'd best stay clear of thar awhile. Tryon's men are bound to be…"

Mary grabbed Christian's hand and ran leading him up the road with renewed strength, fueled by the last stages of exhaustion as weariness converted into desperation. Where the road touched the trees that edged the meadows of Holt Plantation, Mary suddenly halted as if striking an invisible wall. For there, several yards beyond, stood a group of tired and tattered men—leaders of the Regulators—surrounded by militia and redcoated officers. Peering from behind a tree, Mary strained to see their faces.

"We'll have your names now, ye rebels!" announced a leftenant, dismounting and withdrawing paper, quill and ink from a writing kit. But no one spoke. "Well, ye have names, I suspect? Even dogs have names!" Still no one responded.

A major leaned over in his saddle and whispered something to Tryon, who smiled and nodded, then rode forth and asked, "Be there a Captain Messer amongst you?"

Christian squealed, "Paw! Hit's paw they're talkin' about!" Mary put her hand over his mouth and struggled to hold him still. So eager was he to risk all and run to his father, that she had to fall with him to the ground and strain to subdue him.

"Shh! Shh!" she repeated. "Hush, Christian! We have to listen! And watch!"

BLOOD AT ALAMANCE!

"If Captain Messer will come forth and show himself, the balance of you may be granted more mercy than might be forthcoming to men of your current station." Tryon gloated on realizing a major figure among their leadership was well in hand.

Robert made a move to come forward from the standing group of prisoners, but was restrained by his fellows. As the battle was in its closing stage, Robert had been assisting a wounded Regulator from the field and into the woods. He helped him astride his own horse and was about to mount with him, when he looked back and saw another wounded comrade struggling to escape. Sending the one ahead on horseback, Robert ran back to the field barely in time to help the second to his feet, and make but three or four paces before being surrounded by men loyal to Tryon. His uncommon valor was shared with the men who were now his fellow prisoners, as most of them were leaders of the Movement. Now they could only lead themselves to stand for right, to the bitter end.

"I could order each of you executed where you stand," Tryon threatened.

The muffled words of "No, Robert," could be heard amongst the captured men as Robert struggled to break through the huddle, and present himself tall and proud before Tryon.

"I am Messer," he announced with confidence. His back was straight, his shoulders squarely back, and his honest eyes unashamed to face any man. Tryon winced at this display of courage—of noble leaning—from so common a man. Fanning snarled at Robert until he slowly turned his head to cast his deep and questioning eyes at him; Fanning blinked suddenly, and looked away, himself likewise embarrassed to see such fine spirit and decency in a man whom they had just been trying to kill.

"Now, Governor, will ye let these men go? Back to their homes and business. I am the only one you..." Robert offered.

"Blazes and brimstone!" Tryon growled. "You ought not to have brought them into your web of treason in the first place—nor the net that now ensnares you!"

TURNER

Fanning, emboldened again by Tryon's reliable domineering, turned in the saddle and asked, "General, by your leave. Might I suggest we remove them from one another and interrogate them separately, and learn of the plans and whereabouts of their co-conspirators who yet remain at large?" Fanning practiced his best facial impersonation of a stern and confident officer, which began to slip and quiver slightly upon Tryon's delay in responding.

Following an uneasy pause of several moments, Tryon finally replied, "Hmmph. Very well. March the prisoners to camp and hold them under guard. Keep them a reasonable distance from one another, but well in hand."

As they moved across the grassy field, Mary and Christian clung to each other in the bushes and sobbed bitterly. As she loosed her embrace on him, Christian blurted, "We gotta take Paw these vittles, Maw!"

"No, Christian, no!" Mary screamed, as Christian grabbed the tow sack and ran from the woods, toward the men.

"Paw, Paw!" Christian called repeatedly, fighting through the sobs choking his voice. He ran to the midst of the men and handed the sack to Robert, fell to his knees and clung to his father's leg, sobbing into the cloth of his breeches.

"Why, Christian!" Robert answered, in a blend of joy and horror. "Why, my brave Christian! Lord bless ye, son!" He concealed the sack of food inside his shirt, lifted Christian and hugged him to his chest, neither one being able to speak a word as their bond of love assuaged somewhat their mutual gloom—not enough to dispel it; just enough to give light a momentary dominance over dark.

Fighting back a flood of tears, Robert then sat him on the ground, placed his hands on his shoulders, and told him with as much reassuring calm as he could muster, "Now, you hurry on back to Mother! I'll be home as directly as I can! And you big boys tend to the critters, ye hear?"

He gathered all his energies to form a smile for Christian's sake, hoping to buy at least a brief delay in the gloom that could soon overshadow the little boy's life. Then

BLOOD AT ALAMANCE!

with a farewell pat on the head, he managed to spit out, "And a hug for little Mary-Ann!" He turned to hide the torrent of emotion now overpowering his face. A sour, sickening feeling erupted from his heart and flushed into his mouth, as genuine peril for his family's security now became clearly possible.

"Here, you! Boy!" called an angry foot soldier, pulling Christian from Robert. "Begone with'ee!" He slung Christian away, incensing Robert and the other prisoners, who quickly stood between the soldiers and Christian.

Soldiers now turned their muskets on the men, one of them yelling, "Hold fast, there! Or we fire!"

Robert answered with, "Let the young'un be, and we'll march on!" The distraction provided time for Christian to run back toward the woods, and to his mother's waiting arms. So eager had he been to see his father, he had failed to notice the carnage strewn about the field. Nor had Mary focused on the physical horror until now. She ran from the wood line and picked him up, hiding his eyes as she ran past corpses, blood and body parts, the aftermath of the melee. She fought back the urge to scream, as terror flowed from her eyes in the form of gushing tears.

Stumbling from his size and weight, Mary now sat Christian down, exclaiming, "I swan, you're too big for carrying now!" Again they embraced, rocking and sobbing on their knees in the bushes for several minutes. At length Mary arose and said, "Let's walk on toward Hillsborough, son, and see what can be done."

"I know Paw's a good man, Maw," said Christian, after a few minutes. "And he's done a good thing, ain't he, Maw?"

Mary nodded and choked back her sobs, answering, "That is right, son. He's the best of men, and he and the others have done the best what's ever been done for our people hereabouts."

Mary looked for distraction from the overpowering grief now embracing them. As if to divert their attention, she took a breather. Sitting down on a boulder, she unfastened and straightened her hair, and tied it back again. As she was straightening her dress and inspecting her shoes, she said, "Now, Christian, brush the dirt off your breeches. You look a sight!"

Knocking debris from his hair, she went on, "Now, we've got to get back and see about the young'uns, and supper. What d'ye want for supper, my young man?"

Christian looked blankly at her, his expression a mixture of love and suppressed fear. As their chins began to quiver, he fell into her arms for a long, silent hug. Minutes passed before she added, "C'mon now, we'd best be headed home." She gave him a peck on the forehead and reassured him with the words, "Hit'll be alright. Bye-n-bye. You'll see."

"But can't we at least go ask about Paw an' them? Over in Hillsborough, maybe?"

After some reflection, Mary smiled and answered, of course we can, little man!" She rubbed his brown hair again, and patted his head. "Of course we can! We gotta hurry, though!"

Careful to avoid the open road, they trekked on within the woods just off the thoroughfare. They would seek concealment whenever they heard the galloping hoof beats of soldiers' horses, then take up their course again toward Hillsborough. They had made little progress when suddenly from behind wide oak trees emerged three young militiamen, one of whom commanded "Halt!" while all three leveled their bayoneted muskets at them.

Mary and Christian clung to each other as they faced this newest uncertainty. Emotion met emotion as the three young men slowly lowered their muskets, and relaxed their tense postures. They were the same troops who had mercy on James Few, allowing him to flee the murderous designs of Col. Fanning.

"What're ye doing here? And where'ye headed?" asked one soldier.

Christian blurted out, "We're a-headin' to Hillsborough, to save...", but Mary covered his mouth and completed answering for him, "We were a-headin' for Hillsborough, for a visit, but hit appears this wouldn't be the day for that!"

"Well, where's ye horse? Or carriage?"

"How do you mean?"

BLOOD AT ALAMANCE!

"Why, that's at least eighteen miles, Ma'am!"

Mary looked down with embarrassment, then sorrow returned to dominate her face as she looked upward again, hugging Christian closely. "Why are ye so concerned with us? We're just common folks."

"Well, I beg forgiveness, Ma'am. I have to ask. But ye be right, t'ain't the day for it. Hillsborough is—shall we say—closed for business for the time being, and ye'd best turn back home. General Tryon has ordered the entire countryside be searched for Regulators, and if ye know any, ye'd best be turning them back, too!"

"I saw prisoners being taken from the field," Mary boldly went on. "What's to become of *them?*" She allowed her tense shoulders to release and slump, and dropped her hand from Christian's mouth.

"Well, uh," the young trooper stammered. "Can't say, 'zackly. Or, ain't s'pose to say. But there'll surely be trials, and word'll get around as to when, and where."

"Well, I thank'ee for that," Mary replied, calmer now.

"Well, yes'm," the boy-soldier confirmed. "So, best to be on about ye way, lest things get worse." He tipped his hat. The other two nodded politely as mother and son ambled away from Alamance in a melancholy retreat to their farm, turning their backs, if not their minds, from the scene of horror for a time.

Nearer Hillsborough, another straggler was not quite so fortunate. Solders struggled to lug a new captive through the woods and into the village streets; a man not so physically resistive as he was mentally incapable of complying; not heeding their commands and dragging his feet aimlessly. For these men had just recaptured the unfortunate James Few.

CHAPTER TEN

S **EARCH** parties began to sweep the countryside. A large detachment had ridden to Herman Husband's house at Sandy Creek only to find he had fled, but confiscated several papers before burning his house and trampling his crops. Men chased chickens and geese, while cattle were driven from the pastures toward the main encampment. A curious leftenant ruffled through the armload of papers written by various hands. These documents were bundled and expedited to Gen. Tryon's temporary headquarters in Hillsborough.

Col. Fanning accepted the papers on behalf of Gen. Tryon, and shuffled through them curiously as he walked into the townhouse commandeered for Tryon's command center, and toward the table serving as his desk. He stopped and grew stiff as a statue when he realized that among the documents were letters to Herman Husband from James Few. He clutched them to his chest in a moment of sheer elation, his face radiating the first genuine smile his surly face had managed to conjure in a vastly long time.

He fought back the urge to whirl about with glee, and turned his face so no others in the makeshift office could see the rapture so evident on his countenance. Then he looked about furtively to make certain no one could witness him inspecting the contents of the letters before Tryon could see them. He read intently now, the ebullience gone from his face, gradually being replaced by a solemn focus. One of the pages held particular interest for him: A letter wherein James appealed to Herman to find some legal means of rescuing Cordelia from Fanning's clutches.

With widening eyes he pored over the lines, "Fanning is holding my betrothed, Cordelia Ownbey, against her will.

BLOOD AT ALAMANCE!

We must aide her escape! Can you enact legal means to seize him and free her to safety? Heaven forbid the things that could be happening to that dear, fair girl. She must be a nervous wreck, as much as I. Please obtain the legal force necessary to rescue her, before men are compelled to take matters in hand." This one he quickly folded and tucked into the breast of his uniform. His face, which had initially paled on discovering these lines, now reddened with rage.

He sat at a table across the room from Tryon and continued sorting the letters, rapping the fingers of one hand on the table while papers fluttered in his nervous other hand. He read on until he found enough incriminating evidence to possibly implicate James and Herman without an accusing finger being pointed at himself. Once he felt confident in presenting the documents to Tryon, he cried out, "Why, listen to this rambling rubbish! James Few speaks of his having *'been ordained to the mission of ridding the Province of North Carolina of the hounds and scoundrels now plaguing the land,'* and being *'born to the high calling of helping Herman Husband bring Tryon and Fanning and their dog pack to the dust.'* Few's as good as hanged!" He slammed his fist into the papers.

He shook with fury as he stormed over to Tryon and laid them on his table. "General, begging leave, but I feel Your Excellency would most urgently wish to witness these flagrant pieces of evidence I confiscated from among the personal effects of the outlaw, Herman Husband!" He leaned back with a clear grin of satisfaction on his face, likeunto the proverbial cat who had finally cornered the mouse.

Tryon read intently, his eyes widening more every moment, until he ultimately erupted with, "Confound it, then!" He banged his fist onto the table. "Why could we not have had this evidence months ago, and thus expedited his hanging!" He rose from his chair and stormed back and forth, his hands clasped behind his back. "There's a fine mangy hound to present to the King! We finally have Husband where we want him, yet we do *not* have him! How did you ever let him escape?" Fanning's snide grin diminished into a quivering frown. Tryon bellowed again, "Well, there will be an example set this day, regardless! Fanning, find this henchman of his, this James Few, and bring him here immediately, without fail!"

Fanning nodded somberly, as if painfully aware that his social standing with Tryon had eroded by his again being addressed as Fanning, rather than Edmund.

Before he could respond, he was distracted by a loud scuffle in the street as a wild man attempted to pull loose from the soldiers escorting him, being struck and bullied for no greater crime than merely not understanding what they wanted of him.

"But why—why are you taking me. What've I done?" the man wailed.

"Why didn't ye come when we called out to ye?" a Redcoat corporal growled. "And why couldn't ye..."

"I didn't hear—I mean, I didn't understand..."

"Yer under suspicion for ignoring our order!"

An old woman called to the soldiers, "Turn him aloose! Don't you'uns know? He ain't right in the..." She paused with embarrassment; but as the men marched on unaffected by her entreaty, her plea became emboldened by pity. As she ran to catch up, she continued, "...he's tetched in the head. Not of his own fault. He's been hounded to it by..."

The woman was brushed aside by collision with one of the sentry's shoulder as the little mob passed. Their captive grew silent now, except for an occasional inaudible mutter as he stared wild-eyed at the scene, obviously disoriented and confused. "Let him go!" came her last appeal. "He couldn't answer you'uns on account of he's..." But her words fell on deaf ears; deafened by cold hearts.

Fanning looked out the window and saw the ill-fated fellow being dragged through the street, and alerted like a pointer on a game bird. "Few!" he exclaimed under his breath. He wheeled about toward Tryon and gleefully announced, "My General, I have already taken that measure, and now provide Your Excellency with the

BLOOD AT ALAMANCE!

aforesaid outlaw, *James Few!*" Returning to the doorway, he called, "Bring the dog in here, men!"

"Never you mind," howled Tryon, rising from the table and approaching the doorway. "If he be a dog, do not assess to bring him within this gentle house!"

Tryon walked onto the porch and eyed the man over, with the curiosity a butcher gives a cow before the slaughter.

He turned to Fanning and said, "Colonel, were it not for his tatters, bruises and grime, one might almost be inclined to think he came of nobler stock than supposed."

"Uh—sir?" For once Fanning was at a loss for words.

"He appears as though he might have been of a higher position at one time, or potentially so. Clothing was once of a better grade than that of the peasantry. I say, *once* was. Intelligent features, except that he now exudes the semblance of a blithering idiot."

"I assure the General, it is the same Few we seek. A farmer of moderate means and education, turned renegade against King and colony," Fanning tossed in.

Tryon now turned squarely toward James and bluntly called out, "Are you James Few?" James looked blankly at him. "Come, now, man. I command you to give an accounting of yourself. *Are you James Few?*" James could only stare at the ground.

"I assure you he is, General," Fanning intervened, grinning like a pauper who had just won a great prize. "He has been a continual source of difficulty in Orange County—and disruptive of Your Excellency's rule!"

Tryon turned again to James and growled, "See there, Few? Colonel Fanning himself has identified you! You, who might have meant so much to North Carolina's prosperity, are but a traitorous swine, and unfit to live within His Majesty's province!"

As if a brief moment of lucidity fell over him, James stood upright and shouted, "Fanning! You be the traitor! A traitor to humankind! A poison to every good thing that ever graced my humble life!"

Fanning stood erect with rage, fists clenched at his sides, and barked, "Bind him tightly, men! Lest he escape as he did this morning! He is a madman with the devil at his side, able to vanish without warning!" He flexed his face and body as if again rehearsing manly gestures in his parlor mirror. His bark sounded more scared than vicious.

"What about Cordie? What has been done with my own dear Cordie?" James begged aloud, through his sobs.

"Hang the treasonous dog!" shouted Tryon. Remove him hence, and hang him, post haste!"

"Without trial, Governor?" asked a civilian onlooker.

"Hang him, too!" shouted Tryon, jabbing an accusing finger toward the interceding man, who ran to his horse, mounted, and rode swiftly away.

"After him!" bellowed Fanning. "And double the sentries on this door!" He followed Tryon back inside, who was trembling with fury. Mounted men made a half-hearted attempt to race through the streets in pursuit of the man, but soon gave up the chase as he entered the protection of the forest.

James' guards dragged him up the street to the nearest tree, fitted a noose about his neck, and stood him atop a keg. The rope was tied to a tree limb, and another was tied about the keg. On command of "Seize the line—stand ready—*heave!*" the line was yanked by four soldiers, sending James off his perch and into the next world—a world surely far less troubled.

Without another thought upon the subject of James Few, Tryon set busily about the task of organizing his troops for the next stage in his campaign of terror. He dictated a list of marching orders to be sent to every company commander. One special order read thus:

"A bounty shall be paid every soldier who brings forth the following spoils: A firearm, 10 shillings. A cow, 20 shillings. A horse, 30 shillings. Any cash or transportable objects of value, to be surrendered to Headquarters for application to the Provincial treasury, with equitable bounty to be paid thereon in tangible goods."

Back in the command center Tryon announced to his staff, "I see the present campaign must be protracted. Be prepared for quite a number of days afield."

BLOOD AT ALAMANCE!

Fanning seemed distracted and less attentive than the other staff officers on hand. Despite his innate cruelty, he looked peaked after his hanging of Few, apparently having less stomach for the vile deed than he had presupposed—and likely experiencing the acute fear that Few's last words concerning Cordelia might arouse an unhealthy degree of curiosity on the part of witnesses. He approached Tryon with a salute and stated, "General, I humbly request a brief leave to see about certain factors concerning the health of servants at my plantation. Moreover, to procure vital supplies to augment the campaign. I can return promptly."

Tryon, in a rare state of calm, even pleasantness, replied, "Certainly, Edmund. And bring back a ham and, if your hives have already been collected, some honey! And should you have none, find a farm that is in need of paying a fine or penalty by the same—*currency!*"

Fanning beamed with a combination of pride and relief at again being addressed in the familiar form, Edmund. "By all means, sir. I shall report back on the morrow, bright and early, said commodities in hand!" He rendered a parting salute which Tryon limply returned, his eyes cast downward now, looking over the Herman Husband documents again.

Cordelia moved about the plantation house in one of the moderately stylish dresses Fanning had recently presented to her. Her hair was put up, giving her neck some relief from the warm weather. It also gave her a degree of pleasure in disobeying Fanning's directive to wear her hair down, an imposed act of simulated intimacy. It was a passive act of resistance against Fanning's increasing attentions of late; indeed, against Fanning in general. She and one of the black servants, Ellie, sat in the kitchen shelling peas. Ellie kept looking downward at her work, visually avoiding Cordelia. Occasionally Ellie would steal a glance at Cordelia's superior attire, and react with uneasiness, again casting her eyes downward.

"What is it, Ellie?" she asked her at last, her soft whisper of a voice always soothing on the ear.

"Nothin', Miss Cordie," Ellie sheepishly replied.

TURNER

"Now, Ellie, we're friends, aren't we? You can tell me what is troubling you." Ellie went on quietly with her work. "It's the dress, isn't it?" Still no response. "Please don't think poorly of me for wearing it, Ellie. I would never put on airs, when I am a servant like you. Every time he brings in new clothes, he takes my old ones away, so I have to wear them."

After some visible uneasiness, Ellie finally permitted a few feeble words to seep from her mouth. "Just don't seem right, Miss Cordie. This is servant's work. You're more than that. You oughta just leave it to me!" Her head gently swayed side to side.

Cordelia patted Ellie's hand reassuringly, which caused her to react with both surprise and satisfaction; her face nearly wincing at the shock of this unexpected kindness, while a faint, humble smile evidenced itself on her young lips momentarily.

"We serve under the same roof, Ellie. Might as well be friends!"

Ellie smiled broadly now, but then seeing the field hands laboring through the window, slowly began to frown and look downward again.

Cordelia went on in her lilting tone, "Did you know my great-great-*great* grandparents came to America as slaves? Well, sort of." Ellie's eyes grew wide as she again shook her head. "Well, they were indentured servants for four years. That's how they paid for their boat fare to America. Of course it was nothing compared to—uh—well, you know. But they could be sold or traded, and had no liberties at all. For four years, at least." After a pause, her eyes appeared to focus on some unseen object far away as she added, "Sort of like me, at the present."

"My Mamm', she died a-workin' in the fields, 'long-side de menfolk." She closed her eyes and hesitated, then tearfully continued, "I gots it too good, 'pared to her. But I am thankful, too. Thankful that you..."

She was interrupted by hoof beats approaching the house. She ran to the front windows and espied Fanning coming up the cobblestone drive. Running back to the kitchen, she said hurriedly, "Quick, Miss Cordie. Massa's home," and began to help her take down her hair. She ran to Cordelia's room and fetched a brush and smoothed it out for her, just as Fanning was turning his horse's reins over to a servant.

The two young women clutched in a mutually supportive embrace, tears falling upon each other's sleeves. In moments they heard Fanning's boots coming up the steps. Cordelia pulled a handkerchief from the cuff of her dress sleeve and mopped at her eyes, patting Ellie on the shoulder in reassurance that all would somehow be tolerable.

"I need refreshment, and my boots off," Fanning called through the house. Hearing no one, he called out again, "Ellie. Cordelia." Ellie ran into the room and poured him a glass. "Well, Cordelia? My boots?"

With a mixture of embarrassment and consternation, Cordelia slowly replied, "I'll fetch Indigo. More decent for a man to do." Indigo was an outdoor servant who mostly tended to the stables and tack, but was allowed into the house for some heavier chores.

"Not Indigo, not in the front rooms! Probably smells of horses and leather. Get in here and…"

"I'll do it, Massa Fanning," Ellie volunteered, straddling one of his legs backward and commencing to pull on the boot.

"Not for a lady to do, Ellie! Not a-straddled like that. Here, let me help you!" Cordelia interjected.

"Lady?" Fanning retorted, surprised at the term.

Ellie dismounted. "Abitha, come help in the parlor, please," Cordelia called through the house. The older servant Abitha appeared swiftly and silently, as if she had been lingering in the shadows in fearful observance of the potentially volatile Fanning.

The three women stood at his feet and tugged together until first one boot was off, followed by the other.

"Dat be all, Massa Fanning?" Ellie sweetly asked.

"Come, Ellie, we have to finish shelling the peas so Abitha can finish dinner!" Cordelia announced, leading her by the elbow.

TURNER

"One moment, Cordelia," Fanning said. The women all stopped and looked back at him. "Ellie, Abitha, you go on about your duties. Cordelia, a word with you." Cordelia faced him squarely, expressionless. "First off, you need not be touching the servants, nor saying *please* to them. Secondly, you need to begin thinking upon a higher station in life for yourself. Continue to train yourself in the refinements of society, and you may someday find your status elevated."

"Yes sir," she dryly replied, turning to walk away.

"Cordelia! Wait..." Cordelia stood in her tracks, not turning about to face him. "...oh, nothing. Go dust my library. You may find something worthwhile to peruse in there. A wealth of culture lives in those books."

Her beauty and emerging refinement attracted him more every day; every moment. He longed to introduce her to society as his own permanent fixture, though forever frustrated with the notion of being married. The noble concepts of loyalty, sacrifice and commitment were uneasy to him, if not repulsive. And now, though she did not know it, she was free of any hope for James Few. Fanning had seen to that this same day. He rolled his glass back and forth between his hands as he pondered how to break the news to her in a manner that would not implicate him. Harder yet would be convincing her that she could be his woman.

Ellie and Abitha served the evening repast in awkward silence, keenly aware of the tension permeating the air. Cordelia was sullen and withdrawn during dinner; not that Fanning had never experienced such moodiness from her. But he wanted to draw her out.

"Any news hereabout, in my absence?" he cooly asked. She toyed with her dinner and did not reply. "There's been much ado about Hillsborough, since Alamance." Still no interest. "I must be off to rejoin General Tryon on the morrow. Could be gone for a fortnight—perhaps longer." He tinkered with his glass, tipping it against the edge of his plate, looking for any response from her. None was forthcoming. Then looking squarely at her, he continued, "*Miss* Cordelia. Our own dear *Miss* Cordelia. I

BLOOD AT ALAMANCE!

may have something of interest to share with you upon my return. An idea for a—shall we say, for a *venture* of sorts. It may greatly interest you. But, more on this, come morning." They finished their dinner in silence, and the evening passed away uneventfully.

Fanning arose before the roosters next morning. Readied for his departure, he spent a few minutes pacing outside Cordelia's door. He went then to his study and began to write out a note to her, "Cordelia, when I return, please be prepared to discuss..." Roosters began to crow, announcing the birth of a new sunlit day. He was certain he heard Cordelia beginning to stir about in her room.

Wadding up the paper and tossing it away, he resumed his little marching drill outside her door, stopping twice as if to knock, then pausing again. The draft from his movement opened the door a mere inch. Peering through, he watched in earnest as she sat before the mirror, brushing out her luxurious hair. Its brightness competed with the sunlight now coming through her windows.

Hearing his horse being led to the front door by Indigo, he finally rapped on her door, edging it open a few inches. She looked startled at his reflection in the mirror, but did not turn around. Folding her hands on her lap she awaited his unwelcome words.

"Cordelia," he began at last. "I need to depart now." He paused for what seemed a lifetime. She cast her eyes downward and again awaited. "Cordie—if I may address you as Cordie—well, I want you to take charge of the servants in my absence, see to any business that may arise..." He coughed to cover his stammer. Could he be about to reveal true emotion for once? "...any business that you are qualified to handle, that is. And take good notes should anyone bring messages or business matters that require my attention."

"Yes sir," she meekly replied, as if hoping that would end the interaction and he would be on his way.

"And," he continued, "I may have a matter of keen interest to you, to discuss on my return." She sat in continued silence, her body beginning to tighten with tension. "Well, um, that is all. See to things." He went out and mounted his horse, and rode away toward Hillsborough.

The lovely sunlit day drifted by pleasantly and uneventfully. Along toward noon Cordelia looked out the kitchen windows to see Indigo in the back yard, hat in hand, and sadly addressing Abitha and Ellie on the porch. Ellie shrieked, and would have fallen off but for Abitha's quick arms. "Oh, dear Heavens, have mercy!" cried Abitha, then repeatedly wailed, "*Oh*, mercy—*oh* mercy!"

Cordelia ran out to the porch, drying her hands on her apron. "Why, whatever has happened, Abitha? Indigo?" Their mournful faces simply stared at her, as tears began to gush. Abitha helped Ellie to sit up against the column, as Indigo ran to fetch a gourd of water.

Abitha rung her hands as her face reflected genuine torment. "Oh, Miss Cordie," she bawled, "word jes' come by one o'the hands over to the Simpson place…"

"Yes, well?"

"Oh, Miss Cordie, yo' man James, he were driv' plumb outta his mind by all what Massa done did to 'im." Cordelia put her hands to her mouth and gasped. "Yessum, an' den jes' yestiddy mawnin', dat debbil Tryon done had 'im…"

"Had him *what*, Abitha?" Cordelia shrieked.

"Miss Cordie, oh Heavenly mercy—dat Tryon done had 'im *hung*, fer nary a reason! He be gone now, Missy. I's so sorry. Oh, Lawd bless ye, honey! He gone!"

Cordelia fainted dead away, falling headlong off the porch. Indigo caught her and Abitha said, "Quick, brang 'er up hyar on de poach! Sit 'er in dat rockin' chair. And fetch some cold water."

By now Ellie revived and picked up the gourd. "Here, dey's still some water in dis," she said, offering it to Indigo.

"Naw, I'd best fetch her own gourd to be a-drinkin' from," Indigo answered.

"Nope, she won't mind a-drinkin' atter me." Ellie stood and carried the water over to Cordelia as Indigo and Abitha looked on fearfully. "We be friends. Missy said so." Ellie sprinkled water on Cordelia's face, and rubbed some on her lips. "Second time hyar lately she done fainted on

BLOOD AT ALAMANCE!

dis hyar same poach—and on account'a what Massa done did to her beau, James."

CHAPTER ELEVEN

LATER in the afternoon, after languishing for hours on her bed in abject grief, Cordelia, wearing her hair up now, emerged tying on a bonnet and pulling on gloves, and called Indigo from the back porch. "Saddle me up that bay mare," she declared, softly but most seriously. "Please. That one over there." She pointed to the north pasture. She turned back to the door and picked up a valise, setting it on the porch's edge.

Indigo and another servant, Grover, stood staring over the pasture fence. A long pause of silence was broken by Indigo. "What Missy got in mind?"

"I'm riding to Hillsborough. Now would you please saddle up the mare." Her face was all cried out. No emotion; just a blank stare and monotone voice.

"But Miss Cordie," Grover spoke nervously. "We gots no side-saddle fit fer a lady."

"Never you mind about that. I can ride however I need." Her gaze and tone seemed focused on a mission, something she needed to tend to elsewhere.

"But Missy," Indigo continued. "Massa gone blame us fer dat, if you goes off on his hoss." He seemed to sense that she was not coming back.

Cordelia thought a while, then went on. "You're right. No call to get you all in trouble. Very well, hitch up the buggy, please. One of you can drive me to town, and bring the rig back here. He'll never know how I left."

Grover lifted her valise onto the carriage as Indigo assisted her in climbing up to the seat. Indigo sat beside her and gave a gentle slap of the reins; they were off. Once they turned out of the stone drive and onto the dirt road, Grover brought out a broom and swept away the wheel tracks which clearly showed where they had entered the roadway.

BLOOD AT ALAMANCE!

Seeing some wildflowers by the way, Cordelia said, "Rein up here a moment, Indigo, if you please." Seeing she wanted down, he dismounted and ran around to assist her. She gathered a large bunch of the native flora and they resumed their ride.

On nearing Hillsborough she again asked Indigo to stop the carriage. "I'm getting out here. Thank you so much."

"But Missy, how you gone git home?" Indigo asked, much concerned.

"Home? I haven't a home. I have nothing. Fanning saw to that. Well, I have just enough money for coach fare to New Bern. I have an aunt there. But that's our secret!" She handed Indigo six pence. "I wish I had more to give you. Buy a special little treat for you and all the servants." Then she began to sob. Indigo fought back tears as she went on. "I couldn't tell the others." She was gasping for air between sobs now. "I didn't have the heart. Please explain to all of them, and…"

Indigo removed his hat and creaked out somber words, as his eyes flooded. "Now, Missy, dat's aw-right. Dey'll know. I'll tell 'em."

She straightened up, wiped her eyes and face gently, and whispered, "You'd best be getting on out of here now!" He nodded sadly, remounted the carriage, and drove away. As she tearfully watched him disappear, she stiffened and regained her composure, and began to walk toward the center of town.

She asked everyone she saw on the streets, "Do you know where they took James Few?" Every time she received only a frightened shake of the head. "Where is he buried? Does anyone know?" An air of silence hovered over the town, a fitting wake for the tragic departure of her beloved James.

Approaching the center of town, she meandered through the several townsfolk milling about, when through them she suddenly discerned Fanning coming down the steps of the townhouse-turned-command-center. Her blank stare turned immediately to one of focused wrath; then owing to her naturally gentle temperament, her eyes transformed into a sweet sadness. Yet her rage did not

TURNER

escape her entirely, as one hand gripped the handle of her valise rigidly, while the other fell to her side, clutching the wildflowers.

With a cool courage that arises only from the heat of desperation, she began to approach him as he barked orders to soldiers on his left, then on his right. She continued to walk in a straight, dedicated line with her reddened eyes fixed upon him like a grip of steel.

His mouth fell open on seeing her, as he stammered, "Why—Cordie! Um, Cordelia! Whatever brings you..."

Another quiet, focused pause, and then her entire soul erupted from years of pent-up ire as she shouted, "Where is he?" She began to hit him about the face and chest with the flowers, now screaming repeatedly, "Where is my James? Where did they bury him? Or did they have the decency to?"

She continued to flail away at him, crying loudly as he struggled to hold her still and to silence her mouth with his hand. Seeing the townsfolk react with disapproving shock at his handling of her, he released her and attempted to quiet her with soft words. "Cordelia, I have been so saddened at this turn of events. I was going to come tell you..."

"Well, where have they laid him?" She sobbed softly now, her head down. "You can at least have the decency to tell me that!"

Offering her his handkerchief, he replied, cooly now, "Why Cordelia, If only I knew! It was the Governor's doing. That is all I know!" After a pause, he walked her over to the side and asked, "How did you get to town?"

"You only need to worry about where I'm going from here!"

"Hmm?" His mouth parted again.

"Dusting your study, I found my papers of indenture. My release date was two months ago!"

"Bu-bu-but..."

"And there is plenty of evidence to suggest you never had the right to indenture me—or that my father owed back taxes at all!"

BLOOD AT ALAMANCE!

"Cordie! Dear, sweet Cordie! You are mistaken!" He conjured an enormous, fake smile and attempted to take her by the arm, but she pulled away. Then his façade of chivalry shed like a snake's skin, as he growled out, "I can send the law after you!"

She turned about and retorted confidently, "That can work two ways, you know." She then stuffed the flowers into his open tunic and said, "Here. You can put these on his grave. After all, you helped put him in it!"

She went over and sat on the steps of a mercantile store, gathering her breath and wits. She went inside and inquired about the possibility of coach service coming to town in the near future.

By May 19th Tryon's forces were mobilized and bound for Salem. Hundreds of Regulators, real or suspected, were taken captive, their crops trampled, houses not personally coveted by Tryon burned, fruit trees cut down, and flocks and all useful goods taken to supply his army. Every farm, homestead, and plantation en route to Salem fell victim to the plunder and destruction of these marching locusts.

Finding the Moravians there still loyal—or at least, confirmed to have taken no part in the rebellion—Tryon camped near them for two days, enjoying the bounty of confiscated goods, and reveling in the aura of what he assumed was a great victory of Napoleonic grandeur. His unending greed for spoils and revenge provided some solace for the inner knowledge that he had suffered severe humiliation at Alamance. But he kept that re-emerging specter's head suppressed by pushing it under the waters of his subconscious, ever filling the pool with material plunder, inhuman cruelty, and constant massaging of his ego.

He continually paraded the dozen principal prisoners around in chains before his troops, and through the villages they entered, calling them his "*scarecrows—men who had appeared frightening upon first look, but turned out to be less than men.*" Whenever his troops reached the homeplace of any known relative of these leaders of the Regulator Movement, he exacted his revenge on them as well, destroying or robbing all they had, and leaving them entirely destitute.

He had his "scarecrows" chained behind wagons and compelled to march for hours and days as he toured in force through the counties of Stokes, Rockingham, and Guilford. If a man fell, he was dragged on the hard and stony road. Others were often too feeble to help a fallen man up, though they struggled to do so and usually succeeded at length. If not, he was beaten by Tryon's more loyal troops until he did get up.

The campaign was far-reaching, and unprecedented in distance and devastation. "A final and lasting impression must be indelibly made upon the errant minds of these rebels!" Tryon would rant. Throughout the land he had his newest proclamation read aloud: "A pardon shall be granted unto all rebels who lay down their arms, and take an oath of allegiance prior to the 10th of July next." Fearful of losing all, hundreds came forth.

The deep goodness of these people could never be fathomed by a ruthless tyrant the likes of Tryon, let alone appreciated. It was their nature to hold a vow sacred and permanent, even when exacted from them by compulsion, and most of them would go to the grave before violating a sworn vow. Had he been able to comprehend that such virtuous traits existed within them, and developed a truly cooperative relationship with these colonial subjects, he might have cultivated a far finer and more productive society and economy than heretofore seen within this or any other empire.

For now all he had was their grudgingly sworn oath to obey his commands, to abandon any future hopes of regulating government, and to pay whatsoever taxes his regime may deem necessary to exact from them. He had their unwavering word, but not their hearts.

Despite the willingness of the people to accept his terms, Tryon went on plundering and killing and destroying families entrusted to his care as their governor, with his evil affinity for keeping the scales of justice and humanity tipped out of balance.

BLOOD AT ALAMANCE!

"For every mile, a traitor!" Tryon announced from the saddle. "And for every traitor, a tree!" And thus the hangings became more frequent, and more random.

Soldiers were dispatched to every house to demand payment of cash and goods for the support of the army. As they crossed Abbot's Creek, Tryon elected to encamp on pasture lands bordering the Yadkin River, a few miles south of Lexington. Men set about slaughtering some of the sixty confiscated cattle and cooking them on open fires. Foraging for food and loot continued at all times.

When Tryon was served dinner in front of his tent, he summoned Capt. Benjamin Merrill, one of the scarecrows. Merrill was pulled and shoved in chains until he came before Tryon, hardly able to stand from weariness and hunger. Tryon, feasting on fresh beefsteak, pretended not to see Merrill. After taunting him awhile, he looked upward at him and snidely remarked, "Hungry, Merrill?"

Merrill nearly swooned with hunger, but was bolstered by sudden rage surging through his veins. This was his plantation, widely known for its beauty and bounty. And Tryon apparently knew it. He also knew Merrill was one of the most respected men in the region, and an inspiration to all Regulators.

"When you undertook to "regulate" me, *Captain* Merrill, your land and holdings became forfeit to the Crown." Tryon pointed a fork at him, likewise jabbing at him with his cold, piercing eyes. His icy, cruel tone turned to a scorching growl. "And when you dared turn your militia company hostile to me, and assumed the audacity of marching them to battle against me, you forfeited your life, dignity, and any claims thereunto."

Merrill stood silently, degraded on his own land, yet maintaining the dignity of the respected planter, captain, and church deacon that he was.

"Three hundred men you mustered to march against His Majesty's representative, Merrill! And though you arrived too late to join in the fight, you're as guilty as those who did. And you'll hang just as quickly."

TURNER

"Following a trial, at least, one would suppose," the statuesque Merrill finally spoke. "Not that a trial necessarily be fair in this province."

Tryon fairly trembled with wrath as he jabbed an angry finger toward Merrill. As if in harmony, two militiamen's bayonets likewise nudged against his ribs.

Tryon motioned for his dinner setting to be taken away, and called out, "Bring forth the evening's cases, to be tried! And stand Merrill aside. He may as well witness the swiftness of justice."

A poor man with ragged clothes was brought up. "Charge?" asked Tryon.

"Vagrancy, Your Excellency," replied a leftenant. "Loitering about in public, with no visible means of support. Claims he be a displaced tenant farmer, yet no man comes forth to speak on his behalf."

Tryon nodded to officers on his left, and on his right, and slammed his hand down onto his table. "Guilty! The fine is five shillings. But of course you haven't it about you."

"Why—why, no, Gov'ner. I've never seen the sight of five shillings in my life! And seldom have I met a shilling."

"Very well, confiscate all he has about him. And apply twelve lashes, well laid on! Take him away! Next case!"

An elderly man was brought forth. "Charge?" asked Tryon, mechanically as before.

"Hiccoughing loudly and rudely as Your Excellency passed on the roadway," answered the leftenant.

A nod to the left, a nod to the right, the slam on the table, and the *de rigeur*, "Guilty! The fine is 10 shillings. Learn to respect your betters!"

The man stared blankly in disbelief.

"No funds about you, I presume," Tryon blurted.

"We gave all we had to your soldiers, when they came for contributions!"

"Impudence! Twelve lashes, well laid on, and banishment from the county! Next case!"

A dozen such "cases" were tried and sentenced. It was an evening's entertainment for a sadistic despot. Tiring at last, Tryon yawned and said, "You'll be wishing one of these lesser offenses was *your* case ere long, Merrill!" He

BLOOD AT ALAMANCE!

looked to the side and saw Merrill had slumped to the ground, unconscious from exhaustion. He said to one of his orderlies, "Give him enough table scraps to keep him alive. He must live, in order to die as aware as fate intends him to!" Scraps from Tryon's plate were dumped on the ground near Merrill.

Turning to a pair of officers, Tryon said, "There now, major; captain. You see how it's done. Take over for now."

Several soldiers put small bells on the horses and turned them loose to graze on the lush green pastures of Merrill Plantation. Well after dark, the quartermaster got word of Merrill's large apiary and ordered several men to go rob the hives for their honey. Some of the hives got knocked over, resulting in massive swarms of bees. Horses, spooked by the bees, began to gallop about with their bells ringing, while men shouted and ran in every direction—either dodging bees, or pursuing errant horses.

Several of the officers and men, already asleep in their tents, were startled awake at the tumult. "Tis the Regulators!" shouted Tryon. "Every Regulator and his brother descends upon us! To arms!"

The shouting of "Regulators!" and "To arms!" continued to ring throughout the camp until every man was astir. Fanning was so shaken up he tripped over his cot, and then his sword, falling repeatedly until finally emerging from the tent, hobbling around as he struggled with his boots.

Everywhere the comic scene was repeated, until some men began to fire into the dark without orders at every sound of hoof, foot, or voice. Just as quickly, shouts were heard from the dark of "Cease fire!" and "Friend, friend!" Finally, an officer was clear-headed enough to order a bugler to sound Recall, which slowed the fracas down.

Tryon was livid at the calamity, and a good half hour elapsed before the clamor died down entirely and the camp returned to good order. Countering the embarrassment of thinking he was under attack, Tryon thrust back his shoulders and boasted to Fanning, "Never saw the like of such foolery, when I led regular Royal troops! Why so many men who fashion themselves soldiers would assume we were surrounded by uncouth invading hordes, is beyond me!"

Fanning replied, "Indeed, Sir! Very much so!"

As Tryon approached his tent, he observed Merrill sleeping on the ground, his chains staked down.

"I took the liberty, General, of tethering your dog outside your quarters," Fanning scoffed.

"Tossed him some bones, too, I see, Colonel," Tryon answered with a satisfied grin. "Too fine a plantation for the likes of him. Whoever heard of a dog as master of a plantation?"

Fanning looked at Tryon expectantly and suggested, "Perhaps, Your Excellency, it should be granted to someone worthy of it; say, someone who has earned it in loyal service to his King!"

Tryon reflected a moment and replied, "Quite so, Edmund. Quite so." Fanning could not restrain a broadening grin, which fell and quivered as Tryon added, "I shall petition His Majesty to bequeath the plantation to my wife and posterity." Fanning reacted as if had been shot. He walked away a few paces, feeling sick.

Merrill had awoken in time to hear these closing remarks. As he reflected on his losses, and the coming misfortunes of his family, a silent tear plowed a downward path through the dirt on his face.

CHAPTER TWELVE

MARY Messer worked wearily at her daily chores, worry governing her every expression, even when she feigned a cheery countenance for the sake of her equally concerned children. And though they would cling to her and tightly grasp her hands in a show of appreciation, they could see through her sincere, love-borne efforts at comforting them.

"Aren't we good people?" Mary-Ann would ask. Her mother would nod in the affirmative. "Then why has such a bad thing happened to us? And our Paw?"

Fighting back a flood of tears, Mary would stroke her hair and answer, "Sometimes bad things happen to good people, because good people can turn bad into good. That way, there is less bad in the world!" Both would then break out sobbing, embracing and crying until they were simply too tired to cry any more.

So far as possible without appearing forward, Mary would inquire of every passerby for news concerning the prisoners taken at Alamance. As before, the flow of information was intermittent and at times self-contradicting. But a constant theme began to evidence itself in the hearsay that Tryon's bloody campaign was over, and trials on charges of treason would soon commence in Hillsborough.

In actuality, the process of trying Regulators had already become a major industry for the time being. Of the hundreds captured, and who had not been hanged on site, dozens were being dealt with at court. Tryon stayed in town, observing and manipulating the process, permitting show trials to proceed in order to get some attention off himself and to make the Regulators appear to be criminals. But he simply could not pull his finger from the pie. The Riot Act, which he had manipulated through the Assembly months before, temporarily made rioting an act of treason, a capital offense. Now that the Act was to expire in nine months, he was eager to push as many men to the gallows as possible.

He stormed over to the court one day, bristling as if he were apt to have a fit. He confronted Judge Henderson and his fellow justices as they were returning from a recess. "What do you mean, allowing two prisoners to have a day of grace once their trial was underway?" he roared. "Are you not aware, we have but nine months in which to try rioters as traitors? And many are still at large!"

"But Your Excellency," replied Henderson, "They needed a day to summon witnesses!" Henderson's bearing shone forth as a true judge and stalwart lover of the law. His long, narrow face presided over a jaw set solid as stone, ruled by a long marble-like nose reminiscent of a Greek column. His air of impartiality and authority were by no means stony, however; within his breast beat a heart, if only slightly palpable, of goodwill overall.

"Witnesses? Bah! What good came of that?"

"*Some* good, Governor. Their witnesses completely proved their innocence!" Tryon seemed helpless against the firm confidence of Henderson's judicial visage, motivating him to rant on all the more.

"You mean to inform me, sir, that the two were not hanged?" Tryon began to turn red in the face.

"Uh—no, Governor. We are not in the practice of hanging innocent men!"

"Impudent! Impetuous! If I say they are guilty, who are you to say otherwise? Of all the unthinking—why, 'tis treasonous to—why…" Tryon was stumped for the moment, by this unexpected encounter with impartial jurisprudence. He banged on the bar until his hand tingled. Rubbing it with the other hand, he continued fuming. "I send you prisoners, and you justices declare them not guilty! What is the use of even holding trials, then?"

"Indeed, sir!"

"Indeed! Indeed! I want convictions, and I want executions. I could have done your job for you myself!" Tryon stormed out of the courthouse, bumping into guards

BLOOD AT ALAMANCE!

bringing in new prisoners and plowing through the crowd of onlookers, impervious to the ripple of astonished expressions he was causing.

"Indeed," Henderson muttered to his colleagues, rubbing his chin and reflecting a moment. The three shook their heads in analytic disbelief. All those years of enforcing Tryon's evil tax exploitations were coming home to roost, now that His Honour Henderson was seeing firsthand the true nature of the tyrant he had been supporting.

"Shall we resume now, Your Honour?" the bailiff asked.

"*Honour*, indeed!" Henderson again shook his head slightly. "Yes, recess be ended, gentlemen. Next case."

On June 12, Becky Nix's husband, Moses, rode up to the Messer farm in his wagon. He had just returned from trading with the Cherokee in western North Carolina. He raised his weathered hand to wave at Mary who was hoeing in the garden, practically watering it with her tears, whose gentle but steady flow never seemed to ebb. The children ran from their places of work and play about the farm, to greet the approaching wagon.

Moses was a wiry, aged son of pioneers, a frontiersman with enough adventurous tales to fill volumes, if only a scribe could ride beside him on his many wagon trips. He twanged out his words with a disarming old Scots-Irish whine, wrapping the listener in a tapestry woven by words; every single word being consciously felt, mulled over, and presented individually like a mosaic tile, until all the spoken pieces presented phrases that held the listener fairly captive.

The harness reins were worn where his hands had held and manipulated them endlessly, a match for the seat of his breeches worn thin from countless days on the wagon seat. He wore an old tri-cornered hat that turned suddenly downward toward the front, almost as if it were hinged. A couple of small holes were visible at the top front, where a bee was crawling in and out.

"Met a man on the road who says they's a-holdin' trials at Hillsborough," Moses declared. "Or, commencin' to."

"So the campaign is over?" asked Mary, wiping her damp face with her apron.

TURNER

"I reckon Tryon's nigh et up all that the countryside could produce fer 'im, and he's got on to other business."

"Court-martial trials? Is Tryon in charge of the cases?"

"Naw, they put Judge Henderson back on the bench, and they claim he'll hold criminal court."

"So, at least Tryon's killing days'll be nigh over. Ye reckon?"

"He'll be around, though. Hit's one thing ye can count on!"

"I've just got to be there, someway or another." Mary began to wring her hands.

"Well, I'll be a-headin' that way, directly, soon's I fetch my trade goods on home. Got to get 'em off the road afore the Sheriff's men find reason to take 'em! All this regulatin' business has kept Tryon's gangs away from the west roads fer a spell, that be one good thang. I'd ruther face Injuns and panthers back thar, than them scoundrels! I allow Becky'll be a-wantin' to come, too. Why don't ye ride with us thar? All of ye can go!"

Mary thought awhile, nodding slowly, then finally answered, "We'd be much obliged to ye, if ye could carry us there, Moses!"

While he was away, she thought more on the matter, and again determined it would not be advantageous to have all the children present at Hillsborough in case things went awry. When Moses and Becky arrived in the afternoon, only Mary awaited them at the road. "My neighbor JoyEllen Arnold has come to stay with the young'uns awhile," she explained, as she climbed aboard the wagon and seated herself in back behind Moses and Becky. "And her husband Steven'll look after the crops and critters a spell."

Christian tugged on JoyEllen's skirts and whispered, "I've got business in Hillsborough, too!" Before she could respond, he ran up the road and jumped from an embankment into the wagon.

The three adults suddenly turned to look at him, startled. "Why, Christian!" Mary exclaimed. "You get on home, you hear?"

BLOOD AT ALAMANCE!

Christian began to weep bitterly. Moses stopped the wagon. Through trembling lips Christian pleaded, "Maw, maw, please—let me go! I gotta go! Please, *please*…"

Mary finally shrugged, looked at Moses, and nodded for him to go on. She beckoned for Christian to come sit on her lap as they cuddled quietly. "What am I going to do with you, my boy. We can't turn around to take you home now."

They arrived in Hillsborough by early afternoon. Men in chains were being conducted to the courthouse, while similar men, already condemned, were led out to meet their fate; the ebb and flow of dim destiny. Moses reined up his wagon as his passengers strained to see and hear through the commotion in the street. They sat patiently listening and observing for an hour. Finally Mary could stand it no more, and got out and worked her way through the crowd to better listen at the open door. What she heard made her wish she had never come. For she heard the judge reading sentence for some of the condemned:

"Ye men have been found guilty of treason, and are hereby sentenced to the Four Horrors of a Traitor. Ye are to be taken hence, strung up by the neck, then forced to watch as ye are disemboweled, and thy bowels burnt before thee…"

Mary sat right down on the ground by the steps, holding her abdomen as if she were going to be very ill.

"…thereupon to be beheaded, and thy bodies quartered, the sundry parts to be hanged from posts about thy native villages as a testimony against thee—and may the Lord have mercy upon thy souls."

A sergeant ran down the courthouse steps crying, "Make way! In the name of the Governor-General!" He ran up the steps to Tryon's temporary headquarters, saluted the officer of the guard, and announced, "Leftenant, I beg to inform the Governor that the traitors Pugh, Merrill, Matear, and Messer are now on the docket!"

Wheeling about before fully returning the salute, the leftenant started through the doorway with the news when Tryon stood from his table desk and gleefully said, "Never you mind, Leftenant. I heard!" He practically pranced out

TURNER

the door and down the steps, then came to an abrupt halt to see these men, objects of particular hate to him, being forced along in chains toward the courthouse. Had they been men? Their appearance was now so bedraggled, one would be challenged to assay an element of humanity about them.

At the same time Christian arose in the wagon bed and shouted, "Paw! There's my Paw!" The Nixes could not restrain him as he bounded over the wagon sideboard and darted toward his tattered father. Clinging to his leg, he cried, "Paw! Paw! They'll not hang ye! I'll not let 'em!"

Tryon, already gawking at the unusual display of fallen folk heroes humbled before him, was again astonished to see Christian now run over to him and fall on his knees, hands clinched together. Mary was right behind him, falling prostrate on her face, sobbing into the ground, muttering through the muffling earth, "Please, please, have mercy on my good husband! I pray!"

"Enough of this—this shameful exhibit! To your feet, woman!" snarled Tryon.

"Oh sir, please, do not hang my father!" cried young Christian. "If ye must, hang me in his place!"

"Who is you father, young lad?"

"Why—Captain Messer, sir! Oh, hang me in his place!"

"Who put you up to this? Tell me!"

"No one, sir! Only I done it!"

"Then, why do you do it?"

"Because, sir, if my father dies, my mother will die also, and all her children will starve and perish!"

Tryon hesitated a moment, rocking on his feet, his face appearing uneasy but calculating in thought. "Bring me Captain Messer!"

The guards maneuvered Robert through the crowd as Mary rose from the ground, flinging her arms about the husband she had not seen for weeks. Christian struggled around until he found a place to cling onto as well, and they embraced him as if they would never let him go.

"Messer," Tryon said, disturbing the momentary air of hope. "You come before me a traitor. There are those present who apparently deem you less reproachable, at least within some narrow dimension of your existence. You may speak."

"Governor, not at any time have I rebelled against our King. I be a loyal subject to His Majesty, as my family be. All I request is my God-given right to raise my family in peace and dignity, and to have our grievances be fairly heard, as His Majesty would surely so warrant."

Tryon continued to calculate. His face appeared as though he were plotting battlefield strategy, though on a more personal level. The throng tensely awaited his words.

"You may do something to preserve your family, Messer. And yourself." Then looking back down at the pitiable figure of sobbing little Christian, he said, "Lad, your father shall not hang this day." Mary and Christian could not mask their sudden exuberance. Even the crowd encircling them struggled to conceal their budding merriment over the emerging turn of fate.

Tryon went on, "I shall release you, Messer, under the condition that you find and bring back to me one Herman Husband, outlaw and enemy of Province and King!" Muffled gasps fluttered through the crowd. "There be now a standing reward of one hundred pounds sterling and one thousand acres of land for the man who brings me Husband, or Rednap Howell, dead or alive." More gasps. "This pledge of property does not extend unto you, Messer. Thus to secure your hasty return, I shall imprison and hold hostage your wife and child, here present!"

Gasps turned to moans as the entire assemblage stood in shock. Even the most loyal soldiers appeared stunned by disbelief. Mary handed Robert a bundle of food wrapped in tow linen, then she and Christian clung to him fiercely as he encircled his strong arms about them. Guards began to pull them apart.

"I'll be back to ye, afore ye know it," Robert said to his beloved wife and son, projecting the courage and hope they desperately needed. But inside, his soul cried like a rainstorm, pierced with the thunderbolts of rage, to think of the present plight these innocents must endure. The devil Tryon had cast him and them into their own separate hells. Robert comforted himself by thinking only God could cast souls into hell, and not the devil, and somehow this manlike devil, Tryon, would surely have to lose his grip on Godly people.

"Goodbye, Robert—go with God. We'll be a-waiting for ye," called Mary. Christian could be heard sobbing over the din of the crowd, "Goodbye, Paw! Hurry back!"

"My love to the young'uns! Tell 'em I'll be back directly!" Despite the crowd of onlookers, the brave and stalwart man let his tears flow freely; for they were not an object of shame, but a sign of the purest devotion to the dearest of causes: his family. The silent testimonies of the assemblage spoke well in acceptance of his effusion of tears, inasmuch as there was not a dry eye among them.

Guards pulled mother and child toward the jail, as others dragged Robert out of town where they removed his chains. He was instructed to journey northward.

Robert set off at a slow stroll, rubbing his sore wrists where shackles had so long been, his senses numbed by the day's horrific events. As soon as he was out of the sight of soldiers, he stepped off the road and knelt in silent but earnest prayer behind the screen of trees. He poured out his soul in grief until alerted by the approach of plodding hoof beats and creaking wagon wheels. He stood and peered around a tree until seeing the wagon was driven by his neighbor, Moses Nix.

For a brief moment Robert forgot his troubles, as he stepped onto the road and hailed him. "Moses! What on earth!" he exclaimed.

Moses reined up and smiled. "Well, thar ye be, Robert!" he answered exultantly. Robert propped his hand against the wagon as they started to speak. But words would not come. Their eyes welled up and each looked away with discomfiture.

Moses cleared his throat and continued. "I been a-lookin' fer ye, Robert. I seen what they done to ye in town." More silence. "Well, look'ee hyar, I can carry ye a spell, 'til ye sort out some plans. Appears ye be bound fer the Virginny Road."

"That's the way they aimed me. They allow Herman took off the same way."

BLOOD AT ALAMANCE!

"So, ye don't even know where he be?"

"Got no idea. Reckon he went as far north as the road would carry him. I'd vouch he doesn't even know what a wanted man he be!" Conversation ceased awhile as the earth rolled slowly by.

"Ye need a horse, Robert. I know where ye can get a-holt of one, a little over an air's drive toward Cedar Grove. I'll take ye thar."

"I'd be mighty obliged. Thank'ee, Moses. Can't pay ye, though. Wisht I could."

More time elapsed before they spoke again. Moses sat uneasily, struggling with inner feelings that needed to escape. "Hit's *me*, what owes *you!* Robert, I's the one what brung Mary and Christian to Hillsborough. Why, if t'weren't fer me..."

Robert snapped out of his sad fixation, jerking his head toward Moses. Overwrought with self-consciousness, Moses reined up and looked squarely at Robert. "Hit was her own request, Robert. And we had no idea how things would go."

Following a long, agonizing pause, Robert looked again toward the road ahead and nodded. Moses continued, "I left Becky back thar in town, to wait on 'em, and see what could she do to get 'em outta thar, maybe." Another long pause passed. "Anyways, Robert, I know where ye can get yore hands on a good horse, no charge, just this side of Cedar Grove. We'll be thar, directly."

"No, hit's *me*, owing *you.* Hit was good to see 'em." Robert's spirits sagged again on reminding himself of their plight, and realizing that he may never see them after today. His morale plummeted repeatedly each time they passed a burnt-out farm house, or a destroyed crop, the aftermath of Tryon's evil dealings. The occasional stench from a hanging corpse by the roadside or in former farm yards gave Moses the impetus to slap the reins and speed his horse up a might. Leaving the scenes behind did not expel them from Robert's mind, however, and he struggled to fight off a sense of guilt attempting to creep over him. Finally he could take it no more, and declared to Moses,

TURNER

"Hit was Tryon's doing! Not mine, nor anybody else's! Only he could've prevented this!"

"Amen, I know," Moses softly replied, patting Robert reassuringly on the knee. "Robert, remember Jarrett Turner, the wounded lad ye helped atop yer horse after the battle?" Robert again twisted his head toward Moses. "Well, he lived, bless him, and saved yer horse from Tryon's men, in the bargain!"

"Where?"

"He rode ol' Atticus straight from Alamance to his grandpaw's little farm, just up the road a piece, and hid out. Why, sha, Tryon never even seen the little place, so tucked into the woods and all. Without the tax rolls in hand, why, ye'd never know the place existed!"

"Are we near the place now?"

"Right nigh. Hit's the home of Franklin Ensley, a friend of the Movement, and whose farm is yet unmolested. Now ordinarily, some might've suspected him fer that, as being favored by Bully Billy. But he's so well thought of, nary a soul questions where he stands."

Robert's sullen face lit up at the marvel of it all. But the light dimmed from his expression again as he asked, "Moses, if word of Jarrett and Atticus got clear across the county from here to you, then who else knows about this?"

Moses smiled and winked, "Franklin's my cousin! And the best horse trader hereabouts. He gets around! He brung me word."

"And doesn't get stopped by horse-thieving tax collectors!"

"He knows more trails than a rabbit, and can smell a taxman or Redcoat a furlong away!"

A few more minutes rolled by, then Moses announced, "Hyar's where we turn off." He stopped the wagon, climbed down, and moved some dead brush to reveal a narrow and little-traveled road. After turning the wagon up the little path, he got down again, replaced the brush, and remounted to his seat. They rode through dense forest, the air fertile and damp. The aroma of many plant species, alive and decomposing and punctuated with the dank air, reminded Robert of the forests on his own home place. For

BLOOD AT ALAMANCE!

a moment his reveries took him back to the peacefulness and pleasantry only such a short time ago. Suddenly he pined for those simpler, happy days, which had now seemingly rushed out of his world.

Moses looked at him sideways and saw he was lost in contemplation. He let him dream on as the wagon creaked along the path. They rode until fording a little stream and rounding a bend. The scene grew ever more tranquil, until the peace was disrupted by three young men emerging from the woods bearing muskets, and standing in the road. "Howd'ye do?" asked Moses with a wave and a grin. Then turning to Robert he explained, "They be Jarrett Turner's brothers—Adam, Nathan, and Jesse! And headin' yonder's their wives, Daniela, Cassie and Iris. Just brung 'em some vittles, I reckon." Moses cracked a slight grin as his eyes darted about for any hint of a spare biscuit.

"I recognize the lads," Robert answered, nodding politely. "Bravest of the brave, at Alamance." Tipping his hat slightly, he added, "How'd ye do, ladies?" But the wives were already passing a bend in their trail. Robert's eyes darted up the path, wondering to what other hidden worlds it may lead; or lurking dangers.

"And now they keep watch hyar—like warders of the wood! Well, fellers, ye know Captain Messer—saved Jarrett's hide, he did! We be callin' on Franklin, to fetch his horse."

They rode slowly into the tree-covered yard as Franklin's wife Verdie was tossing out a basin of red-tinted water, a by-product of tending to Jarrett's wound. "Franklin anywhere about?" Moses asked Verdie.

"Why, hello, Moses! He be down yonder at the barn, a-shoein' that black stallion what Jarrett rode in on!" Robert nodded at Verdie as they rode on past the cabin.

Robert's faithful mount neighed and tossed his head up and down as he approached. They were glad to see each other. Robert patted his neck and rubbed his face affectionately, purring to him, "There, boy! Good old Atticus!" After a reflective moment, he added, "I reckon I'll need to change your name to—*Alamance!*"

CHAPTER THIRTEEN

F**RANKLIN** refused any praise for his care of the horse, deferring rather to all Robert and his steed had done for his grandson.

"We wish fer ye a safe and successful trip, Cap'n Messer," he said, his gratitude showing in his face as surely as it was evidenced in his firm handshake.

"Well, thank'ee most kindly for the invitation to stay a spell," Robert replied. "But there's the need to press on. Thank'ee, Miss Verdie, for the comforts of home."

Verdie replied, "Hyar's ye a hasty dinner on the porch, and some ham and biscuits to take with ye."

Robert savored the breakfast, then saddled Atticus—now Alamance—and mounted him as Verdie handed up a little tow sack of rations to take along. He rode behind Moses as they wound their way back through the canopied forest and onto the road.

They never revealed to the Ensleys the mission in which Robert was reluctantly engaged, it being such a sorry business, and bound to taint the goodwill shared during their short stay. Moses had to practically force Robert to take a shilling and sixpence for his needs, which he finally accepted with gratitude. They exchanged parting words, then turned each his own way: Moses to return to his wife in Hillsborough, and Robert bound for parts unknown.

He drifted in thought as Alamance plodded along. So far he was proceeding as directed, but the assigned task was not in his heart to carry out. Now and then they would spook a bird into taking flight, giving Robert pause to think of how free the lowly birds were—free to go where they pleased—and even though hunted by man, could quickly escape without consequence.

BLOOD AT ALAMANCE!

It occurred to Robert that he could indeed escape, and just keep riding onward, free as one of those birds. But just like the birds, he reasoned, he ultimately had a nest to return to, and dependents who would starve without him. And though Mary and Christian may eventually be freed if he kept on riding, their farm would be forfeited and destroyed, and he may never see them again.

There was no peace forthcoming with Robert's temporary release, as he struggled with all the options. And regardless of the outcome of any act he resolved to pursue, there would not likewise be any peace expected. He pondered if Tryon was clever enough to devise such a complicated torment for him on a whim. For certain, he was mean enough. But Robert took some solace in the knowledge that at least he was motivated by love and devotion, traits apparently alien to Tryon. In that respect, he was far wealthier and more powerful than Tryon could ever hope to be.

Riding for some two hours, Robert began to fret about finding water for Alamance, watching carefully for signs of a stream or spring. A half hour before dusk he came to a shallow ford in the road. He dismounted and held the reins as he and Alamance partook of the cool water.

He led Alamance off the road and into a thicket looking for a place to bed down and hide for the night. He was relieved to discover a small grassy clearing in the bushes. He removed the bridle from Alamance, and used the reins to tie a large rock to his hind leg, thus hobbling him to prevent his straying off as he grazed. Then he removed the saddle and placed it on the ground. Laying his head on the improvised pillow, he fell fast and deep into a much needed sleep.

But sleep was disturbed by a series of short, intensive dreams rippling through his subconscious mind-filter. Eventually they would form into one whirling depiction of many fragments of his life: his family at home, playing or working together, with always a sharing of grand smiles—his childhood memories of sitting near Cherokee council fires admiring his father—of county folk firing their light muskets into young militiamen who could have been their friends and neighbors—who convulsed in agony—of soldiers' bayonets piercing the lungs and hearts and stomachs of innocent men. He would toss about, mumbling, sometimes scratching at the ground to remove stones from under him, half-waking for a moment, then falling back into near sleep again.

Once in the night he was startled awake as Alamance neighed, thinking someone may be approaching. Then on realizing the four-legged friend was in want of hydration, he removed the hobble stone and led him by his halter back to the little stream for a drink. Robert stood staring upward awhile at the clear, open skies, contemplating the myriad of stars; each independent and unobstructed by the others, yet all shining in unison for a common purpose.

"The morning stars sang together, and all the sons of God shouted for joy," he uttered reverently.

Alamance curiously turned his heard toward his master, on hearing his voice.

"Lord said that to Job. Wish it was like that down here, *under* the stars."

After anchoring Alamance to the ground again, he laid back down, still looking at the starry sky; then fell to pondering the present condition of Mary and Christian. And the children still at home—who was minding them?

Back in Hillsborough, Mary and Christian had been held at the crowded jail until their housing could be arranged. They were escorted under guard to the home of Arch and Polly Collins, on the south end of Church Street. As they walked along the dirt thoroughfare, Mary could see other leaders of the Regulators being held in an unsheltered camp. Tryon had postponed the hanging of these fine men—James Pugh, Robert Matear, Benjamin Merrill, and now others: Alan Lineberry, and Morgan Stanfield—pending Robert's return.

The lead guard rapped on the Collins' door and announced, "Beg pardon sir, ma'am. These quarters are appropriated by His Excellency, Governor Tryon, for the keeping of these two prisoners—until further notice." Polly stared blankly, and before she could speak the soldier turned away with the comment, "Your claim for expenses

BLOOD AT ALAMANCE!

will be considered, at the proper time." Leaving the doorstep, he placed two guards on the house, gave them their final orders, and left.

Polly nervously motioned for them to sit. They sat quietly for several moments, until Polly asked, "Have ye been to table?" Mary and Christian shook their heads softly, looking downward. "Well, come an' have something. I just set the table for my husband, Arch, an' they's plenty! Come join us!"

The table was set with roasted chicken, cornbread, boiled potatoes, and fresh green beans; good colonial fare. The meal was completed before anyone spoke. Mary did not know what to think of this couple, or if they could be trusted. Finally Arch broke the silence by gently asking, "Hit's about the Alamance trouble, hain't it? We know all about it. We can't speak openly on the matter, but if there's ary a thing we can do to help your situation…"

At last Mary spoke. "Thank'ee, I…" she began. After a pause, she went on, "…more than anything, I need to send word to the rest of my children—to let them know we are safe—for now."

"Oh, we'll get word to 'em," Arch allowed. Arch consented to carry a message to their neighbors Evan and Hilarie Cook, who would be traveling in the direction of the Messer farm on the morrow.

Mary and Christian retired to a spare room upstairs. Through the window she looked down at the soldier guarding the front door, then led Christian to the bedside to kneel in prayer before lying down for a night of fitful sleep. She kept awakening and looking toward the ceiling, pondering Robert's plight and the future of the family.

Once abed, Mary, like Robert, lay awake, troubled over his condition and whereabouts. And like him, Mary longed for true rest and ease of mind, despite the comforts of house arrest. In her dreams she would hear the distant sounds of battle and many men's voices calling, shouting, rallying—then as the roaring calamity neared, she would see Robert coming through a mist until he was in front of her. But as they reached out for each other, he would begin to fade away and drift back toward the din of battle.

Yet at least somewhere in the ethereal realm their souls touched within the eternal bond of family—the unwavering mélange which, if nurtured, would strengthen the community and colony and the entire country, though Tryon did not seem to appreciate the value of this priceless asset in his tearing down so many families.

Sunrise awakened Robert on the hard ground where he lay atop the reeking saddle blanket, with the saddle beneath his head. Sniffing the air he declared, "Old Alamance, my friend, the smell of your gear is less than pleasing!" Then on sniffing his sleeves and the front of his shirt, he confessed, "Pardon, old friend. Appears hit's *me* in need of cleansing!" He went to the stream to bathe and wash his tattered shirt as well as he could without soap.

He hung his shirt to dry on the bushes and sat down for a ham and biscuit breakfast, pondering his pursuits for the day—riding into mystery, whether going ahead or back.

In Hillsborough, morning began with equal uncertainty for Mary, who could hear a dim clamor far up the street as the day's trials and executions continued in full, accompanied by crowds of the curious and cautious alike.

Trials were expedited, with little allowance being given for the summoning of witnesses. All too often witnesses, too, were charged along with defendants for no greater crime than having been associated with them.

In order to expedite Tryon's legalized murders, men being condemned to death by the archaic Four Horrors of a Traitor were finding their sentences lightened to mere hanging. The first attempt to carry out the disemboweling and quartering of a man proved too ghastly for inexperienced executioners; and whereas there were a good many men to put to death, simple hanging became the vogue. Though still horrible and undeserved, at least they were being dispatched to the next world with considerably more ease.

Seeing the day was likely to grow warm, Robert put on his still damp shirt after saddling Alamance and rode onward toward Yanceyville. Despite being nearly two days

BLOOD AT ALAMANCE!

northwest of Hillsborough, the occasional farms or plantations he encountered were still burnt out and devastated, feeding a continual resurgence of gloom and dejection that hung over him like a pall. Trudging along on his aimless quest, he would nod his head in silent prayer for every victimized family whose homes were now obliterated, and whose lives—like his—were distressed in the extreme. "Oh Lord," he would begin. After a troubled pause he would continue, "Have mercy on these men's families. Lift them up and deliver them, for the hand of darkness overshadows them…"

Occasionally he would halt his horse at grassy, shady spots and allow him to graze. He would look up and down the road and wonder why he kept moving onward. What could he accomplish by traveling ever farther up the road? Then he would tell himself that if he could just find sympathetic people who had survived Tryon's raid, he might seek worthy counsel from them that could give him ideas for bringing about a resolution to his quandary. Thus he would wander ever onward, searching his soul for clues. He needed a sense of mission in order to fill his days and hours with purpose. He thereby resolved to at least try to find Herman or anyone associated with him, to seek counsel and—if he were still in the area—warn him of dangers awaiting him.

On reaching a crossroads he saw a man approaching on foot by the road to the left, carrying a scythe on his shoulder. The man stopped on reaching a corpse hanging from a roadside tree, and, swinging the long blade upward, cut the rope and let the decomposing body fall.

The man said a silent prayer over the body and walked on toward Robert, staring blankly. He was evidently displaced and dealing with his own inner torments, likely another victim of Tryon's locusts. As he approached, Robert hailed him and asked, "Which is the best route to Virginia?"

"The right road leads northeast, and the left goes northwest, both to Virginia," he replied, his voice wavering in a ghostly monotone, like someone who had lived too closely to death. "Same distance either way. They's naught

TURNER

of interest whichever ye take, 'cept the left leads through Yanceyville. They's more Indians to the northwest, but they be gen'lee friendly."

Robert knew all this, and knew the Cherokee and related tribes of the area. What he was fishing for was any voluntary information on news, events, and possible sightings of other travelers that would be of interest. Since this information was not forthcoming, he asked outright, "Any news along the way? Meet anybody, much?"

The old man shook his head. "But hark'ee, most anybody ye meet is either a-hangin', a-rottin', or a-robbin'. Ye hain't got a spare morsel about ye, have'ee? Or could ye part with a penny or two?"

Robert unbundled his handkerchief to remove his last ham biscuit and handed it to the man, whose stolid countenance now began to beam with relief. "Oh, thank'ee kindly, neighbor!" He did not hesitate to partake. "Ain't et in two days."

Remembering the coins Moses gave him, he drew a two pence coin from his pocket and handed it down to the old refugee, whose eyes lit up with sudden bliss. He tried to utter words of gratitude, but they would not come forth through his quivering lips.

"Think nothing of it, friend. Hit was give to me in the first place." Presently Robert began to think of purchasing more provisions in Yanceyville, relieved that he need not go hungry after sacrificing his last bit of food. He nudged Alamance onward toward the northwest, leaving the old gent to his own wanderings.

Yanceyville drew into view shortly. Robert was surprised to see the streets of the little village empty. Looking to either side he noticed wary faces peering from windows and cracked doorways. A barking dog was the only voice of greeting he received. The town had little to offer by way of amenities or businesses.

Nearing the end of town, he heard a woman's voice around a corner. Slowing up his horse, he listened intently at her words. "I see ye got another pamphlet, Nellie," she said to someone. The other replied, "Yes, I got it from Amanda Crockett. Her husband Mark picked it up in

BLOOD AT ALAMANCE!

Hillsborough a while back. Sit a spell and I'll read it to ye, Kizziah."

Robert halted completely, and listened as the unseen Nellie's voice read to the unseen Kizziah, *"Tyranny will make a wise man mad, and if you tread on a snake it will turn and bite."*

"Reckon that was one of Herman Husband's sayings?"

"Hit don't say his name anywheres on it, but hit sounds like 'im." She went on reading, *"His Majesty's honor is dimmed when…"*

Robert perceived he may be among friends. Taking heart, he nudged Alamance onward and around the corner, and completed the quote aloud, *"…when the lights of his subjects are put to shadow."*

The ladies appeared astonished and on the verge of outright fear at his sudden entrance onto the scene. Were they friends of the Regulators and suspecting him to be a Tryon ally? Or were they enemies and bent against the likes of him?

"Pardon me, ladies," Robert was quick to say. "Where are all the menfolk? Is there any place about, for the purchase of some feed—for man and beast?" He patted Alamance on the neck.

Nellie hid the pamphlet under her skirts as she rocked on her porch. Evidently distrustful of newcomers, she kept rocking and observing, uttering nary a word. Finally her companion Kizziah spoke up, saying meekly, "Things are unsteady hereabout, for now. What might ye name be, sir?"

Knowing he had nothing to lose, he admitted his name. "Captain Messer. Robert. I'm on an errand…" Robert halted his tongue, fearing he may be perceived as being in pursuit of Herman—whether as friend, enemy, or bounty hunter. The ladies' elevated anxiety evidenced itself in the increased speed of their rocking chairs.

After exchanging several frightful glances at one another, Nellie said, "We've sure heered of ye, Captain Messer." Robert observed the women's expressions closely, attempting to discern if his renown was locally favored, or condemned. "We're not free to talk openly on these things, ye understand. We've already lost a good many of our menfolk, and stock."

Kizziah added, "I can only sell ye a might of feed corn fer ye horse. They's not much left in the crib, 'til crops come in, in the Fall—what's left of 'em. But we'd be obliged if ye could move on, directly, on account of..."

"I'd be most happy to abide by your wishes. But ye needn't fear—I've not brought any trouble with me, and there's none trailing me. But just the same, if I could just buy some grain and maybe a few vittles..."

Kizziah and Nellie swapped calmer glances now. Kizziah pointed across the dirt street and said, "Ride 'round back of the house over yon way. They's a well and a trough. Beyond that's the corn cribs. They's not much thar, and we have to make it last. But help'ee self to an evenin's horse feed. They's fodder in the near crib, feed corn in the middle'un, and the fer crib's fer next year's seed corn."

Apparently Tryon's hordes had ruined the crops just south of town, and neglected to raid the corn storage at this home. *Were these loyalists?* Robert wondered. *Or just lucky survivors?*

Nellie interjected, "And I'll fetch ye some vittles from inside, by the time ye care for ye horse."

"I'm much obliged," Robert replied with gratitude. He started to tip his hat, then remembered he had not had one for days. He shrugged and smiled, then turned Alamance across the street. As soon as he was heading around the side of Kizziah's house, she and Nellie were buzzing with chatter about the mysterious man in their midst. Robert rode into an enclosure, dismounted, and closed the gate. After drawing a pail from the well for the water trough, he removed the bridle so Alamance could feed. He brought an armload of fodder and a few dried ears of corn and laid them in the feed trough. He paused to hear a pig snorting and chickens cackling in the barn, supposing they were being hidden there from Tryon's men. He felt much relieved to deduce that these women were likely akin to Regulators, or at least not aligned with Tryon.

BLOOD AT ALAMANCE!

Returning to Nellie's front porch while Alamance fed, Robert boldly asked the women, "Are you safe here? Did your menfolk suffer at the hands of the soldiers?"

Silent tears made sudden rivulets down both their faces. Holding back an emerging sob, Nellie answered, "My man's upstairs, overcoming a foul wound; Ancel Gillespie. Just thankful to still have 'im! I can call out 'Ancel,' and feel saved from my greatest fears just to hear him answer back, alive. Kizziah here hain't seen her man in two days."

"Not hurt, I hope!"

"No," replied Kizziah. "Just gone to Virginia to see can he buy a wagon load of goods to see us through. But having to travel alone, because…"

"Because so many of our men *are* hurt—or dead—or just plain missin'," added Nellie. "He was too scairt to go a-buyin' near Hillsborough."

"I'll keep an eye out for him, when I leave directly," Robert offered.

"Oh, ye'll have to stay the night, at least! Supper's nearly to the table!" Robert had found living friends in a nearly dead village.

"I'd be mighty obliged," Robert answered humbly. "Oh, and here, is this enough?" he asked, handing two pence to Kizziah.

"Oh, thank'ee! More than enough. I'd not take hit, 'cept—well, things bein' what they are."

"Hit's nothing. Hit's *me*, owing *you*, ma'am."

Robert ate well, and should have slept better than he had for some time; but despite the comforts of roof and bed his sleep was beleaguered all night by recurring nightmares. Even in sleep, Tryon was able to torment him.

Like shifting fault lines beneath the surface, battles arose in his subconscious mind, fought in frenzy for uncertain victory, then left the field for a time—only to return and renew the fight once illusory peace proved fleeting.

The vagaries of images sharpened at times, to play out again and again; scenes such as Capt. Montgomery being blown to bits by artillery—young and innocent boys taking

TURNER

a .69 caliber round through their heads and chests—men and boys with shattered arms and legs screaming to be comforted—and wounded men being burned alive in a dry and kindled forest. All the time he saw himself struggling in vain to save innocent and valiant lives. Wailing voices of troubled faces would cry out to him, as arms reached toward him. In desperation he would grasp at them, but every time they would slip through his hands and disappear.

"No! Withdraw, you boys! Save them! Save them!" he screamed out in the dark, bolting upright in the bed in a cold sweat. He took several heavy breaths and eventually plopped back down again—only to dwell for an hour or so upon the plight of his family. Then drifting off to sleep again, he would find himself reliving the intense horrors that befell his friends at Alamance.

He lay awake for two hours awaiting dawn; he was relieved to see the sun finally make its return appearance. Rising, he found his way down to the kitchen where Kizziah was stirring gravy for her hot biscuits. Her bonnet off now, he could see a fresh red sunburn on her otherwise tender neck, a sign that she had been outdoors tending to chores her missing husband ordinarily performed—tasks to which she was unaccustomed. But in step with frontier spirit, she did not shrink from the demands of survival.

"Get some rest, Captain?" she asked dryly over her shoulder. She knew he hadn't.

Shuffling his feet and casting his eyes downward, he finally replied, "Hope I never disturbed anyone. That is…"

"N'er ye mind, Captain. Hit ain't the first time Tryon's haunted innybidy's dreams hereabout."

Following a quiet repast of biscuits and gravy, Robert reluctantly arose from his chair and went outside to fetch Alamance. The day was clear and sunny, and looked promising. He saw Nellie on her porch across the way, eyeing the street left and right for any sign of strangers.

As he cinched the saddle, Kizziah came out, took him firmly by the arm, and softly asked, "Ye'll keep an eye out fer my husband, Gilliam Souther, wonchee?"

BLOOD AT ALAMANCE!

Robert patted her gingham-clad shoulder and replied through his forced smile, "You know I will. Lord help us all."

"Here, ye'll be a-needin' this." She handed him a spare hat of her husband's. "Keep the sun and wind off ye head and face."

Robert rendered a cordial smile. "Well, thank'ee kindly! Hit sure will be a comfort." He took her hand and shook it warmly, patting it with his left hand.

Mounting and doffing his new old hat to her, and then to Nellie, he turned Alamance up the road. He didn't expect much in Virginia, but hoped it could provide a brief diversion from the horrors still evident in North Carolina. He was just borrowing time against fate's account.

CHAPTER FOURTEEN

BARELY had the ink dried on the document lying on Tryon's desk before catching the eye of Mrs. Margaret Tryon, who had come to pay a visit at his headquarters in Hillsborough. Soon after her arrival, she was eager to depart again for New Bern, on witnessing the suffering and misery her husband had inflicted on the pitiable local folk. Almost every face in the streets bore testimony to recent sorrow as people struggled to adjust to the desolation forced upon them.

"To His Soverign Majesty," the document began, spurring her curiosity. The purpose of the letter was to petition for Benjamin Merrill's plantation to be granted to his own family. She looked about, then with a snide grin took pen in hand to secretly amend the wording. A few editing touches rendered the document a petition for Merrill's widow and children to *retain* the estate upon the demise of Captain Merrill, rather than Tryon, whose tyranny was sowing seeds of rebellion even within his own household. Yet like most ivory-tower autocrats he was not at all attentive to the growing disrespect he was earning.

The last sentence read, '*...and hereby respectfully request and recommend that the estate of the said Merrill be henceforth taken of his heirs and assigned then to yours truly.*' With one fell swoop of the pen she altered it to read, '*...be henceforth a token of his heirs, and assigned them too. Yours truly,*'

Tryon had left his desk to inquire of the mounting noise from the streets. The curious were talking about the status of Mary and Christian, the political hostages. On learning they were being held on house arrest at the Collins' home, a small crowd began moving down Church Street in hopes

BLOOD AT ALAMANCE!

of learning more about them. Tryon instructed his soldiers to break up the unlawful assembly, then bring them to him.

As soon as the people were dispersed, except for a few lingering onlookers standing at a distance, a detail of soldiers arrived at the house to retrieve them.

A young leftenant called at the door, saluted Polly, and said dutifully, "Begging pardon, ma'am. We are here for Mrs. Messer and son."

Polly looked at him, and side to side at his three soldiers, and asked, puzzled, "What is happenin', sir?"

"We've orders to escort them back up to town."

"Well, wait here while I fetch 'em."

The officer instructed the men, "Stand guard at the sides and rear of the house," then paced tautly up and down the front porch.

In minutes Mary and Christian appeared in the parlor. Polly handed Mary a bundle tied up in cloth, explaining, "Just some spare clothes fer both of you'uns. Hope they fit. And a few morsels to tide ye over."

Mary, overcome with emotion, hugged Polly in silence, nodding her thanks as tears again emerged on her apprehensive face.

She stood in the doorway blankly observing the young officer, who came to attention and saluted her. "Beg pardon, Mrs. Messer. We have orders to escort you and your son to headquarters," he stated with polite detachment. He then called out to his men, "Escort, to the front." The soldiers returned to the street as Mary and Christian looked on in surprise.

"Is there some news, sir?" Mary asked eagerly. "Some word of Captain Messer?" Her eyes were riveted on the young officer's face, watchful for any word or expression.

The leftenant shook his head and replied, "Just orders, ma'am. If you please." He motioned with his hand toward town, and they began a slow gait up the street.

"Where're we going, Maw?" young Christian asked, holding her hand and looking up at her.

"We'll see, son," she replied, going on to inquire of the soldiers, "Is my husband back?" No response. "Has Captain Messer returned?" The guards maintained silence. Her anxiety grew as tears resumed rolling down her cheeks. Sensing her trepidation, Christian's eyes now began to swell with tears.

The constant uncertainty in the midst of expectation had worn Mary's emotions raw, well past the point of exhaustion; yet her love for her husband and family—the good, innocent victims in this strange picture of cruelty—drove her instincts to endure. Ever since the Battle of Alamance, she had been living day after day in a dark valley, caught between the ominous peaks of catastrophe and insecurity.

Again they passed the makeshift prisoner camp which served as an overflow area for the crowded jail. James Pugh observed her pass, then continued speaking to Robert Matear: "There be no mistake that I was captured firing on Tryon's men. I downed at least fifteen of them. But why are you here among us? You've done nary a thing—you never even joined the Regulators!"

"Yes, 'tis true, I've committed no violence against Governor nor King. My only offense was to read a sealed letter, nearly three years past!" came Matear's somber answer. Seeing the curiosity in the eyes about him, he went on to explain, "When I entered Tryon's camp to encourage terms of peace, he recognized me, from way back then. Or at least, my name. He never forgets a grudge."

"Why, whatever had you done, that your name would never leave his mind?"

"I was in New Bern delivering a wagon of corn and wheat to market, and he learned I was bound for Salem, my home. He had his men give me a letter to take to the Forsyth County sheriff. After two days on the road, my curiosity got the better of me. I admit it, I slid it open from the side, where it was loose—careful of the seal—and was able to peek inside. I simply had to know what fate he may be declaring on our people by way of that letter! What it said so disgusted me, I couldn't keep it to myself."

"And?"

"Well, truth be told, I talked. Not much, but I did. Then word spread." He paused to clear his throat and his thoughts. "Remember that tale that ran about, of Tryon instructing the sheriff up yonder to double all legal fees, off the record—and take half of all property bequeathed to widows before they could be probated? Well, I told it, and my name was told along with it."

"That makes ye evil and guilty in Tryon's eyes, I reckon," Pugh added. "When ye expose evil deeds, the evil doer marks *you* as evil. Every time."

"Ought not've looked; but he ought not've entrusted it to me in the first place! So here I sit, dishonored and done for." Shaking his downcast head, Matear continued, "Must've been desperate to hurry and get it to the sheriff. But knowing his evil ways, I was desperate, too—to look and see what cruelty he was planning for my county!"

"Condemned for the cause of justice." Pugh shook his head.

"In North Carolina, justice has a different title. Doom is now my name."

Pugh nodded in solemn silence. Then looking toward the street he saw the guards leading Mary and Christian along in the distance. Pointing toward them with a tilt of his head, he whispered, "Yonder be Captain Messer's wife and child now!"

"Where d'ye think they be a-going?" asked Benjamin Merrill. "Surely Captain Messer's not back."

"At least not back with Herman, by any means! Surely not," added Pugh. Then after some reflection, he woefully continued, "They'd not be turning his wife and child a-loose, otherwise—unless he be—"

"Dead? Or a-fixing to be? Lord have mercy."

Mary and Christian were marched up the steps of Tryon's temporary headquarters, and ushered inside. Upon seeing them, he turned away and walked into another room, unable to face them despite having them foremost in his mind this morning.

He remarked to Fanning, "We need them sequestered closer and more securely. But not here, I don't think. Any suggestions, Edmund?"

Fanning leaned to peek out the doorway and into the front room where the Messers stood, eyeing Mary up and down, and with a grin, replied, "I could house them, Governor."

"Nonsense, man! You live too far from town!"

"But I've taken rooms nearby, until the present undertakings be completed. I've ample room there."

Tryon looked Fanning over skeptically and distrustfully, studying his face like a map, perhaps the first time he had ever sized him up so intently. Summing up Fanning's nature and motives came quickly. "No, I shall house them in the servant's quarters, back of this house. It is occupied only by the old cook, presently."

As if distrusting Fanning to carry out his order, Tryon called for a subordinate officer. "Leftenant Stansell," he commanded. "See that the two prisoners are placed in the outbuilding, under guard." Then glancing once more at Fanning, he continued, "No visitors—of any kind." His protectiveness of the Messer hostages was not out of compassion for them, but to abate the growing scandal associated with them which could further erode his posturing of propriety.

Robert rode most of the day, not seeing a single unmolested farm until he crossed the Virginia line. Another half hour passed in leisurely travel, riding slowly to survey the contrasting countryside. Tall stands of trees, mostly oak and pine, bordered the roadway like sentries for long stretches, with an occasional break in the form of meadows or farm fields, followed by shrub land. Then fields of countless cedars, then forests again.

Riding through another swath of shrubs, he heard a rustle in the bushes. He looked to his right to see a musket leveled at his head. He was starting to dig his heels into Alamance to gallop onward until the voice behind the musket called out, "Robert! Ho, Robert!"

Spinning about, he was surprised to see Vaughn Cunningham, one of the Regulators from his own neck of the woods. Vaughn appeared haggard from prolonged exposure to sun and elements. Despite his usual tan and leathery complexion, he looked peaked. His dark red hair hid for a moment a spatter of dried blood, close to his collar which also bore red stains.

BLOOD AT ALAMANCE!

"Well, sha, Robert! Of all the folks to see in Virginny!" he croaked through a strained voice. It was as though his mouth and throat were a dusty cavern, and his words a mere breeze drafting through it. As Vaughn emerged fully from the concealment of the bushes, Robert could now see the lump on the back of Vaughn's left shoulder where a large padding was covered by his vest. Robert deduced that beneath the padding was a sizeable wound, slow in healing. When Vaughn stepped onto the road and attempted to mount his horse, it was obvious he could not hold his musket and grip the saddle at the same time, depending on his right hand while his left arm hung nearly limp. Robert instinctively reached over and held Vaughn's musket while he climbed atop his horse. "There. Thank'ee. Got a festerin' hole in my shoulder, what likes to rein me in a bit."

"How'd ye get hurt, Vaughn?" Robert inquired with sincere concern.

"Took a musket ball across the shoulder. Missed the bone, mostly. Ripped the flesh."

"Alamance?"

Vaughn nodded in the affirmative, wincing with pain. Robert had never seen the rugged man sick and weak. "You need some vittles, or water?"

"I'll make it."

"Which way you riding, anyway?"

"I was intent on escapin' to upper Virginny fer a spell, but now—well, as ye see, I may not be long for this world. I wanted to slip back into Orange County to see if innything was left of my little farm. If they be ary a thang thereabout worth stayin' fer, I might turn myself in to Superior Court 'fore the sixty days of grace run out. After that, I have no rights at all, to property or life. Seems Tryon's took over God-given rights, as if they was his own."

"Hit's a risk, any way ye take, now. How far did ye get?"

"Halfway to Maryland, afore my wound started turning bad."

"What news have ye heard?"

TURNER

"Fer weeks now, all ye hear about is Alamance, the battle, and Tryon's stompin' feet. And Herman Husband a-passin' through hyar."

"You've seen—Herman Husband?"

"Just heered of him, is all. Ever-bidy's been a-talkin' about him passin' through, ever' place ye go."

"Where did he end up?"

"He's plumb gone from Virginny. I heered he be holed up in Maryland, bound fer Pennsylvania now."

"That be good news, Vaughn!" Robert smiled easily and freely for the first time in weeks. "All I needed to hear!" He turned Alamance around and said, "I'm bound for Hillsborough. My business here be done!"

"What *be* yer business, Robert?"

"Just to find some good news! Come on, ride with me. You can get good care in Yanceyville, at homes of friendly folk. They be with us, and Tryon's not apt to return there. Nothing left to steal!"

Vaughn's trust of Robert was apparent, as he nosed his horse back down the road and joined him on his return ride toward Yanceyville. Gradually, subtly, Robert increased Alamance's pace, with Vaughn keeping up. He kept an eye on Vaughn's condition, careful not to risk his comfort or safety for the sake of speed. But as Vaughn was drifting in and out of sleep, his horse instinctively kept pace with Alamance, until they were nearly at a slow trot.

It was late evening before they reached Yanceyville. As Vaughn's horse drifted toward the Gillespie porch, Robert dismounted in time to catch him as he slid semiconscious from his saddle, groaning long and low. The audible anguish wasn't loud like a roaring stream, but rather like the muffled undercurrent that frightens with its runaway strength.

Nellie, spying them through her window, threw her hands up with wide-eyed wonder. Soon the same reaction was being generated by Kizziah Souther. Both ladies ran out to assist, making darting glances left and right to discern if any trouble rode in with the men.

"Better we get 'im over to my house," said Kizziah. "You've got enough on your hands, Nellie, with your man."

BLOOD AT ALAMANCE!

As they helped Vaughn across the street and up her steps, Kizziah went on. "Captain Messer, I don't reckon ye got fer enough to see any sign of my Mr. Souther up yonder way?" Robert could only shake his head in quiet regret.

Soon Vaughn was lain face down atop a bed in the back room, and preparations were underway to tend to his festering wound. Nellie and Kizziah began to remove his vest and shirt. Peeling back his crude bandage they nearly swooned at the sight of his odious infection. Kizziah lit a fire and laid the iron poker in it to heat up. Robert sensed her purpose; his eyes were wide open when they met hers. She responded with a nod, and whispered, "Got to cauterize it. Might be too late, now!"

Nellie ran across the street to her house and ran back with an earthen jug, from which she poured a cup of clear yet pungent liquid, whose contents she forced Vaughn to gulp down. "Hit's just fer medicatin'," she explained. Robert nodded.

Next she splashed some onto a clean cloth and began to swab around the periphery of Vaughn's big sore. He gradually seemed less concerned with his awful state now, waning in his focus and awareness until falling into semi-consciousness, though the ladies seemed more concerned than ever.

Kezziah kept the fire intense. Once the poker was red hot, she retrieved it from the flames and nodded at Robert and Nellie, who took the cue and held Vaughn down while she began to burn out the infection and heat-seal the blood vessels. Robert and the ladies fought off the temptation to faint dead away, their foreheads beaded with nervous sweat. The overpowering stench paled in comparison to Vaughn's horrific scream, which did not cease until the foul but necessary deed was done. The pain was so intense as to propel him from his stupor. Gradually his scream diminished to a pitiable whine, and with a long groan he passed out again.

Another half hour passed before Nellie could say to Robert, "We've heered some talk a-tricklin' up from Hillsborough since ye rode out, Captain Messer!" He turned his focus toward her and listened intently, his eyes drawing

TURNER

out her words like deep magnetic wells. "Word is, Tryon says if ye'er not back thar directly, he's gonna send your wife and boy off to prison, fer good!"

Robert became visibly agitated. After negotiating for some water and feed for Alamance, he fed him and gave him just enough time for it to settle some in his belly, and to take some vittles for himself. He tied a bundle of corn to his saddle, then announced his intended departure. He pulled from his pocket the shilling Moses Nix gave him, and reached it out toward the ladies. Seeing their dumbfounded reaction, he offered, "Hit's the least I can do for all your kindness."

"Now," he continued, "I've got a family to tend to. Please give Vaughn my best wishes, and saddest farewell."

Robert swung up astride Alamance and rode off into the evening toward Hillsborough, taking no time to receive the flood of profuse thanks the womenfolk expressed. As his anxiety rose, it manifest itself in his heels as he nudged Alamance through faster paces, reaching a trot and a canter, then slowing to a fast walk as he realized the need to avoid wearing him out. He rode all night, stopping only for occasional watering whenever they reached a stream or pond.

At first light, Lt. Col. John Bautista Ashe was ordered to detail soldiers to clear a grove of trees in order that viewers could see future hangings unimpeded. The viewers were to be families of the condemned, whom Tryon ordered to witness the deaths of their loved ones. "Let there be not an eye that escapes the punitive result of their kinsmen's rebellious and seditious deeds!" he had roared. Giving orders was one thing; carrying them out in reality was something entirely more difficult. This realization tugged at Ashe's heart, as he had come to sympathize with the Regulators who had captured him shortly before the battle. Now in temporary command of all of Tryon's army, he reluctantly yet dutifully carried out his mission.

The gallows, which had seen much use over the past several days, was nothing more than a beam supported by two posts, under which stood a barrel upon which the

BLOOD AT ALAMANCE!

condemned would stand until soldiers kicked the barrel from beneath him.

By mid-morning, a lone horseman and his tired mount were seen riding slowly into town from the north. He pulled the front of his hat down low over his eyes. No one seemed to notice it was Robert as he maneuvered Alamance cautiously down Church Street, looking for a safe and friendly face with whom he could leave his well-loved steed. Within sight of Tryon's headquarters, Robert dismounted and led Alamance slowly behind him. Eventually he spied Moses Nix helping Becky onto the seat of their wagon, on the right side of the street half a block from the center of town. He walked slowly over to them and whispered, "Moses! Moses, look here! It's me, Robert!"

Moses and Becky jerked their heads to the left, looking startled, and then attempted a smile.

"Robert, hit be good to see ye!" Moses replied.

Becky whispered, "I've done purt nigh all I can fer Mary and Christian, I'm a-feered. Tryon's aiming to send 'em off to prison soon! Or indenture 'em out somewheres."

Robert pressed his finger to his lips and shook his head. He held to the sideboard of the wagon and hung his head in grief, pausing as if to draw the strength to speak. Looking back upward he asked faintly, "Are they in comfort? Being fed? I mean, are they allowing you to get in to see them?"

"Well, yes, but now they've moved from the Collins' house to Tryon's cook's house, I have to take the guards at their word, such as it is, that they be giving 'em the things we brung."

"We were headin' back home, Robert, but can stay a spell longer," Moses added.

"Ye've done so much for us already, I am in your debt. But if ye could manage to take my horse on home with'ee, I'd be eternally obliged."

Moses and Becky nodded. Moses said, "They'll be glad to have good ol' Atticus back."

"Tell my young'uns from now on to call him— Alamance."

TURNER

Robert turned to give Alamance a farewell pat on his neck, and sauntered on down the street, sure he would soon be identified, being ragged and road-worn.

Reaching Tryon's headquarters, he looked around for any way to get past the house and possibly visit Mary and Christian in the cook's cottage. A small crowd observed this new entry onto the scene. He overheard first a man comment, "Hain't that Robert Messer?", then a woman's voice whispering, "Look'ee, thar be Cap'n Messer! I be sart'en of it!" Soon the crowd was buzzing with utterances of "Messer—hit's Cap'n Messer!"

Finding himself now in the midst of curious onlookers, his options were few. When the guards outside Tryon's door took notice of what was transpiring, his options were narrowed to only one: report in.

Climbing the steps, he stood before the guards who came to attention and casually announced, "Please inform Governor Tryon that Captain Messer has returned."

BLOOD AT ALAMANCE!

CHAPTER FIFTEEN

SUNRISE over Hillsborough, North Carolina on June 19, 1771 had appeared much as any other day. None could have foreseen that the day's events would resound forever in history. History begins with little events that build into larger ones—far-reaching ones propelled by destiny, seasoned with the flavors of the intensity and passions and desperation of the human experience.

As Robert stood on the porch awaiting Tryon's emergence from within, he turned to look over the crowd below, all standing in silent awe. Running through his mind were the myriad of imagined possible outcomes of his present act, whirling like a giant spinning wheel, hoping it would stop on the most favorable option: that his wife and child would be released from Tryon's cruel clutches, and that possibly he would be freed to take care of them, for at least appearing to have attempted to locate Herman. His reverie was suddenly interrupted as Tryon burst onto the porch.

"Messer!" Tryon's voice shot through him like an icy steel blade. He looked about, side to side, and over Robert's shoulder. "Well? Where is Husband?"

"Governor, my report is that..."

"*Report?* What *report?* Where is your prisoner?"

"Sir, I know where he has gone. I cannot take him, however, without enough men to surround and overpower him." Though Robert did have a rather vague notion of where Herman could be eventually tracked down, in his heart he could never actually assist in seizing him for Tryon's wicked pleasure. Surely the present circumstances would inspire Tryon to release the Messers unmolested.

But Tryon merely snapped his fingers in the air and shouted, "Hang him!" He called again, "Colonel Fanning, hang this traitor immediately!" Receiving no response, he asked aloud, "Where is Colonel Fanning?" He spun about and strode briskly away to fetch Fanning. As his guards stood to attention at the doorway, he snorted at them, "Forget the doorway! Seize that man, Messer!" Jabbing a finger in Robert's direction, he continued, "Hold him here until Col. Fanning arrives for further orders!"

"But Governor, we had a bargain!" Robert called out, as the guards took him by the arms.

Tryon turned to look sternly at him again. "What's this business? Begging for your life now, Messer?"

"Not at all, sir. But for my wife and son. What of their welfare?" Grief swept over his face and filled his heart. Tryon stared icily until seeing the effect he had had on Robert, then turned his face away in denial. "Governor, what of my family? My good and innocent family?"

As Fanning approached on the porch, Tryon turned to him and snapped, "Bring the traitor's wife and son to the gallows, to witness how we deal with treason! And bring the remaining condemned men as well. Their families are likewise to witness their deaths. Set the hour of execution at eleven o'clock! Order Leftenant Colonel Ashe to form the troops and prepare accordingly!"

Fanning smiled, rendered a snappy salute, and spun about to enforce the order which seemed to please him so.

"*Leftenant* Colonel Ashe," Fanning gleefully called out. "Bring the condemned party and their vile kinsmen to the execution venue. By order of His Excellency, General Tryon!"

As Robert was being tied to a porch post, his hat fell to the ground. Onlookers stared down at it; no one dared pick it up until Mary ran into the mob and retrieved it. Hugging Robert as if it were the last time, she was soon joined by Christian who likewise joined the embrace.

Tryon returned inside the house, only to be confronted by his wife. "William, surely you do not intend to carry out this monstrous act!" she snarled at him with a rapid and forceful half-whisper.

BLOOD AT ALAMANCE!

"Madam, composure!" he responded, in the same fiery undertone. "Come with me." He led her briskly by the arm into his office and slammed the door, to prevent her words of protest from being carried on the public wind. A heated exchange of words could nonetheless be overheard through the closed door.

Suddenly the door was flung open and Mrs. Tryon emerged briskly, her eyes fierce and her countenance quivering with anger. The heretofore icy and calculating disposition for which she was known, showed a crack in the enamel as she allowed herself to express genuine, humane emotion resulting from the atrocities being committed by her own husband. She went out onto the porch and raised her gloves to summon her driver, who brought her carriage up.

At eleven o'clock twelve men and their families were forced along East King Street to the place of execution on Halifax Road. Tryon followed on horseback, arrayed in full military uniform. At his appearance, the full militia was ordered to attention and solemn drums fell silent. Soldiers surrounded the gallows in an outward-facing square.

At the last moment Tryon presented—more as a display of power than of mercy—six names chosen for pardon. With a mixture of pomp and austerity he read aloud from the document he held before him: "Hear ye, all present, and witnesseth ye, that it pleases His Majesty to shew forth mercy upon certain of his subjects, as a sign of the benevolence and goodness with which it is ever his intent to rule. The following prisoners will therefore be recommended to His Majesty for pardon from their sentence of execution this day, to be eventually restored to their families where, it is admonished, they serve their Sovereign King with wholeness of heart henceforth."

Mrs. Tryon eyed him sternly, almost as an expectant overseer. Tapping her gloved hand with her folded fan, her gaze remained fixed upon him as he continued to read.

"Forrester Mercer, James Stewart, James Emerson, Herman Cox, William Brown, and James Copeland—these six, and no more—are to be dismissed from the gallows herewith."

TURNER

The air instantly filled with a mélange of cheers and sobs, incongruencies of heart that blended perfectly with the inconsistencies of the day. As he brought the paper to his side, he was momentarily distracted at the swift departure of Mrs. Tryon, who had entered her carriage surrounded by her mounted escort. Soon they were riding along the roadway to New Bern. "Faster," she had instructed the driver, as if needing to escape the nightmares behind her. Though she held her head high with distinction, the trace of a tear could be seen flowing backward from eye to ear, as the breeze carried it along. The cool statue found she possessed the essence of a heart.

"The aforesaid six shall be held in custody pending the good pleasure of His Majesty, the King. Upon receipt of his wise and worthy disposition, further consideration shall be made on their behalf." The spared men were then pulled from their families and led away to jail pending pardons from the King.

Ashe faced the remaining six prisoners with intense remorse on his face. He whispered to them, "Gentlemen, I deeply regret this action. I would to God it could be reversed." Their faces suggested no anger or resentment, only a tender sadness for the future of their families. Otherwise, they seemed hauntingly at peace.

Ashe avoided their eyes as he read the order for their executions. "Benjamin Merrill, James Pugh, Robert Matear, Alan Lineberry, Morgan Stanfield, and Robert Messer: Ye men, all, have been convicted of high treason and sentenced to death by hanging. Let the executions begin. And May God have mercy on your souls." Cries of their loved ones again filled the air.

Tryon and Fanning looked quickly and angrily at each other. Tryon blurted out, "That scoundrel, Ashe! He did not read my entire text! He left out every word about their worthlessness as subjects of the King, and the great harm they have rendered his Royal province! And what of the Four Horrors—the quartering of bodies? Why, I'll..." Tryon turned as if about to give an order.

BLOOD AT ALAMANCE!

"General," Fanning said, halting him with his hand on his arm. "We have come this far. All present will witness the power and effect of His Majesty's justice—and your superior rule. I humbly submit that we let the hangings proceed without delay! We can deal with Ashe later."

"Yes, I suppose interruption would only feed a notion that we do not have order here!"

Irreversible events were now set in play. The culmination of the perverse fantasy shared jointly by Tryon and Fanning was hurling from the earthly realm into the annals of history.

As the rope was placed about Merrill's neck, he asked if he could sing a hymn; Colonel Ashe nodded approval. As he began to sing "Christ the Lord is Risen Today," Tryon griped, "A Methodist hymn! A rebel to the very end!"

"It is my understanding that Merrill is actually a Baptist," Fanning commented. "These backcountry denominations seem to be standing together, which of itself reeks of treason!" The comment made Tryon nervous, yet firmed his resolve to remove these men from the realm of the living.

After uttering, "Faith in God has sustained me in my efforts to gain dignity for my countrymen," the barrel was kicked from beneath his feet, and the gallant Captain Benjamin Merrill was no more.

Pugh next mounted the barrel. "Have you any last words?" Ashe reverently asked.

Pugh nodded humbly and said, "I stand before you with a conscience devoid of guilt. I am prepared to meet my God; His name be praised. Our blood today will be as good seed sown in good ground, and will produce an hundredfold! I do wish to state that I forgive those, my tormentors and executioners. For I fear for their souls. William Tryon will be held accountable for exploiting and crushing the innocent lives of those who might have served him most nobly. As for Edmund Fanning, my pity be upon him, for his paths will lead to naught but destruction, and thus I pray for his soul to..."

Fanning interrupted his last words by storming over and kicking the barrel from beneath him, sending him to his death. The wickedness of his scowl was equaled only by the cruel smirk on Tryon's face.

Ashe pulled Fanning aside. Gripping the handle of his sword, he growled silently but strongly, "Colonel Fanning, a word with you!" Pulling him behind the back rank of soldiers, he continued to express his keen displeasure. "Fanning, you've no authority! You are naught but a murderous beast!"

Fanning simpered and coldly replied, "We can take this matter up with His Excellency, the Governor-General, at your leisure!" Pulling loose, he moved a safe distance away to continue observing what to him must have been festivities. Gradually overcoming his cowardly reaction to the hanging of James Few, participation in Tryon's murderous campaign seemed to have desensitized any essence of humanity remaining in him, facilitating his taste for the macabre proceedings of the day. Moments later a soldier handed a written order to him, from Tryon: *"No further words from the condemned. Proceed with all dispatch."*

Fanning strode briskly through the mob and ranks of soldiers, and handed the order to Ashe with a grin of evil satisfaction. He then turned to the soldiers and commanded, "By order of His Excellency, the Governor-General, there will be no further words from the condemned. Get this business done!"

Cries of disbelief arose with the wails of grief. The hangings proceeded swiftly. Matear stood atop the barrel, and—seeing his remaining time fleeting like vanishing vapors—hastily got in a brief parting remark: "My crime was to speak against crime. My voice will be silenced, but the voice of God will yet speak on His earth!" His words were cut short as again the barrel was kicked, dislodged from beneath his feet with the cold brutality of the occasion.

"Hang them faster!" shouted Fanning. "Step it up, ye laggards! Heave to!"

Lineberry and Stanfield were dispatched without ceremony, in the blinking of an eye. Robert assumed his position atop the barrel, gaining his first glimpse of Mary and Christian. They were pale and undernourished, and

BLOOD AT ALAMANCE!

had that weary look of being thoroughly cried out. As their eyes met, the bond of love fixed within their mutual sight like a beam of power, overriding their desolation and dread for a golden moment of shared glory; invisible to Tryon and his henchmen, but real and powerful nonetheless. Robert expended the last five breaths of his valiant life expressing and sharing this love, a lasting love that could not be snuffed out by the acts of men, but which would endure forever.

As his heart swelled within his throat, his care for his dear family would not subside, growing ever greater until manifesting itself within the rapidly-blurted words, "My love to Mary and the children! I pray our Heavenly Father grants them peace and joy until we soon meet again!"

No sooner than his words had projected through the air, than he was hanging at the end of a rude rope, rendered physically disgraced, but spiritually glorified. Mary had broken her gaze into Robert's eyes, looking away as the obvious was about to happen—and tried to turn Christian's face away as well, though soldiers manually forced their heads toward Robert. As if by Providence, floods of tears blurred their vision as their beloved Robert's body hung before them.

Robert's lifeless form was taken down and tossed aboard a waiting wagon, to lie among the five others who had gone before him. Transported eastward from town, they were unceremoniously dropped into a mass grave by the Eno River. No mourners or ministers were allowed to attend.

The momentary quiet had been interrupted by officers shouting orders to escort the wagon of dead men, to usher the throng back toward town; and to marshal the streets, clearing them of civilians and dispersing them on their way. Moses and Becky waited in town, looking for Mary and Christian. Seeing them at last, Moses beckoned them over to their wagon. Becky threw her arms around Mary as Moses placed his arm on Christian's shoulder.

They stood in silence for a time, then Moses broke the stillness with the admonition, "Ye'd best be headin' back to yer home, afore they come and take everthang." The harshness of the facts within his gentle statement rang true, and Mary nodded in acknowledgement. He was not being callous, but only expediting the necessary, for Mary's own sake.

With Alamance tied to the back, Mary and Christian sat cuddling in one corner as the wagon rolled away from Hillsborough toward the Messer farm, and to the remaining five children who had not been seen for many lonely days. The place looked the same; it was both a comfort to see, yet a dreadful site knowing Robert would not be there. The children heard the wagon rumbling up the road, and came running from every direction, elated to see mother and brother once again. No sooner than Mary had knelt to hug her children, than Moses and Becky had commenced to carrying belongings out of the cabin and placing them in their wagon.

Another neighbor, Mae Cloer, greeted Mary. She was one of several who had relieved the Arnolds from time to time. Mae read Mary's drained and mournful face, and gave her a long, silent embrace.

"Walter drove the stock to our pasture, and hid the chickens at the Nichols farm," she explained. "County men came a-huntin' for the stock but never found ary." Her husband Walter had also taken the hams and beef from their smoke house, and meal and flour from their pantry, keeping them safe.

Mary stared through a cold and detached countenance, slowly managing to respond, nodding quietly as if it were understood that she would be leaving her beloved home. Becky approached with an armload of blankets to lay in the wagon, and mentioned to Mary, "I know the day is nigh over, but ye'd be better off staying up at our place fer the night." Again Mary nodded, and gathered her children for the wagon ride to the Nix farm.

"I'd best hurry home and fetch some of ye smoked meats and some meal to take with ye," added Mae, turning to hurry to her house.

Bedded down at last at the Nix's house, Mary lay awake all night with sleeping children on her arms, Christian lying closest to her. He would grumble in his sleep

BLOOD AT ALAMANCE!

and awaken at times, but feeling her comforting arm, would eventually drop back off. Just a few winks before dawn, Mary got out to the barn and saddled and bridled Alamance, and rode back toward their farm. There was need of something there that compelled her to a near-gallop. Within a quarter-hour the cabin came into view. She slowed up, and approached cautiously.

Dismounting and tethering Alamance outside, she slipped into the house and plundered around until she found her most prized possession: the family Bible. She clutched it to her chest and walked out onto the porch. She started toward the horse, but then stopped and opened it. She read aloud one last ceremonious verse, in honor of Robert: *"No greater love hath a man than this, but that he lay down his life for his friends."* Pausing for a silent prayer, emotion rolled over her like a sensory tide. But no tears fell. All her tears were expended; there would be no more tears. She honored Robert with her faith and courage in that brief but powerful moment, then, with her family Bible clutched closely, remounted Alamance and rode slowly away.

JoyEllen and Mae had been careful the past few days to move Messers' personal belongings and store them in the Cloer barn. Mary walked over and picked out a few treasures, and utensils and items of clothing they would need for a journey. Moses came over and said, "Let me gather some more neighbor men to brang wagons and carry off ye remaining furnishings, before government men come and take it all."

She politely shook her head and answered, "Thank'ee, Moses, but I reckon not. We'll not be needing any of that." Moses looked embarrassed on realizing she was likely to leave the county. "Please spread the word to folks hereabout, to come and take what they can use." Moses nodded silently. "But better have them come by tomorrow, afore hit's all forfeited!"

After two days of hurriedly organizing for their exodus, she and the children were again riding, by courtesy of Moses and his wagon. They rode slowly atop the wooded crest about a quarter mile above the Messer farm,

TURNER

stopping to observe as loud deputies and soldiers complained about not finding any booty anywhere on the place; then proceeded to torch the house and barn, and to pull down the snake-rail fences. The children were already asleep again, and did not see what Mary and Moses saw. Moses mercifully slapped the reins and they moved on to the west.

CHAPTER SIXTEEN

F**ORESTS** grew thicker and the roads less developed as they rolled ever westward. Farms were fewer and fewer until there were none left at all. By day's end they pulled over to camp by a gentle stream, and caught trout and sought forest herbs and berries to supplement their dinner.

Christian sat closely by his mother's side most of the time, unless she asked him to do a chore or fetch something. Brother Tipton, near in age, tried to tease and taunt Christian into playing or exploring with him. "C'mon, Christian! Let's go look for crawdads in the creek!" he would plead earnestly. But Christian would only snuggle up to Mary all the more, and stare into infinity.

"Now son," Mary would reassure him, squeezing him with her arm." "You don't need to sit around like a knot on a log! Help Tipton gather some firewood, then maybe you can catch us a few crawdads for supper!"

Christian slowly came to his feet and began to look for wood with Tipton. Moses looked over from his fishing and cranked out, "Ye'd best be lookin' fer snakes, too, while yer at it! They's rattlers and copperheads 'round hyar. I've seen many a snake hereabouts!"

Just as Mary Ann came skipping up to present her mother with a wildflower, Mary gasped and called out, "Where's Joseph, and Jarred! And Solomon, where are you?"

"Right over here, Maw," Solomon called from across the stream. The younger boys were tossing rocks into the water. Moses called out, "Easy, fellers! Don't skeer the fish off with them rocks!" They dropped their rocks and ran off to climb in a huge cedar tree. Again Moses admonished, "You'ns be keerful in thar, boys. They's ticks in thar!"

"Ticks!" Mary gasped again.

TURNER

An inner healing seemed to emanate from being surrounded by nature. For certain, there was health and good spirit in the air, the gentle stream carrying on in its innocent passage of time, and the towering, strong trees seeming to impart the wisdom of the ages. Peace and serenity abounded. Four days they spent traversing the wilderness in this manner, until the roads were little more than trails leading up and down ever-steeper slopes. But they were not alone: the woods were gradually filling with refugees from Tryon's reign of terror, and squatters were seen building crude shelters in many places, attempting to eke out a new living; or carving new paths to any hopes that lay west.

Moses knew where the good streams were, and managed to get them to a suitable camp site each evening where good water flowed, and fish and edible plant life abounded.

Gradually Mary met and made friends with some of the outcasts. The womenfolk would swap small amounts of necessities, talk of their vague plans for survival, and eventually would end up sobbing over their common plight. Mary Ann would accompany her to these informal gatherings, and when she would see the women all begin to shed tears, she naturally would too; though she would squeeze her mother's hand and sputter through woeful tones, "Ma-Ma! Hit's alright! Don't cry." They would almost ritualistically hug and return hand-in-hand to their own encampment.

Back in camp, Moses remained aloof, keeping an eye on the exiled men camping near them, his pistol always tucked in his belt and his musket within reach. "Ye cain't be too keerful 'round strange men, 'specially out hyar in the wild country," he would admonish Mary.

"Oh Moses," she would whimper. "Their womenfolk are all the company I've got. And they're bad off as we are!"

"Just keep an eye out, is all."

"And you're keeping your powder dry, I reckon?" Mary surprised him with a sudden but faint smile. Moses nodded and patted his musket, cradled in his arms.

BLOOD AT ALAMANCE!

Then Moses' eyes opened widely as he whispered to Mary, "Don't look jes' yet, but they's somebiddy a-comin' up the trail, behind me."

"I don't see ary a soul."

"Jes' listen. Somebiddy'll be hyar, dreckly."

Moses slowly turned to face up the trail. A Cherokee man stopped in his tracks and peered from behind a tree. Moses rested his musket over his shoulder and nonchalantly sauntered toward the man. As he came within fifty feet of the statuesque visitor, he called out, "Osiyo."

The man nodded and replied, "Osiyo."

Joseph and Jared stopped cold in the bushes to see this strange site: a lean but very muscular red man with long black hair, a bare chest, and loin cloth. His feet were shod with leather moccasins, and his legs were covered from the feet up to the thighs with leggings of red trade-cloth. He toted a long, light musket in his hand, while an antler-handled knife in a buckskin sheath hung from a leather strap around his neck. A head band, arm bands, and wrist bands completed his accoutrements. Four dead rabbits hung from a leather string around his waist. The boys looked on in silent awe, casting glances at Moses to see what he was going to do.

Moses approached him with a stern face, then as he neared, broke out in a broad grin. The Cherokee man suddenly smiled, took him by the hand, and said, "*Moh*-sace! *Moh*-sace Neex!"

Moses replied, "Atohi, osiyo!" He motioned for Atohi to come join them in their camp, but he politely shook his head.

"Must hunt. Must move back before new people take game."

"Yep, I reckon. Wish ye could stay a spell."

"You bring new people to Tsalagi lands?"

Moses nodded, frowning at the ground and then shaking his head in reflection. "Yep, I'm a-brangin' 'em. But jes' this one family. They got no place else to go. Her man, dead. Friend of Tsalagi. Robert Messer."

Atohi's eyes lit up. "May-sah? May-sah dead?"

TURNER

"Murdered by white chief, Tryon." Moses put his hand to his throat and popped his head upward, making a hanging gesture; then cast a quick look toward camp to make certain Mary did not see the act. Thankfully the boys did not, having scurried back to camp to inform the others of their adventure in discovering their unique visitor.

Atohi's expression changed suddenly to grief. He turned to the trees to hide his emotion, then turned again to Moses. "We bring Tsalagi warriors, hunt, kill white chief!"

Moses shook his head. "Thank'ee, Atohi. Too late fer that. Hit would take all-out war, and never git solved."

"Atohi go home now. Here. Take." He removed two of his rabbits from the waist string and handed them to Moses.

"Wado! Wado!" Moses nodded and grinned thankfully. "Wait cheer. I'll fetch ye a little sumpthin' or 'nuther from the wagon, to take home with ye." By the time Moses reached the wagon, he looked back and saw that Atohi was gone, dissolving back into his native woods as an integral aspect thereof.

"Moses! Rabbits!" Mary exclaimed with delight, particularly since Moses had failed to catch any fish. "Did the Indian give them to ye?"

"That he did. A good old hunter-warrior I run into once in awhile. *He* usually finds *me*, though."

"You speak a right smart of Cherokee. Does your friend speak much English?"

"More than most of 'em. He likes to stay in the woods to hisself, but will come barter with the most trusted white traders, and picks up a few words hyar and thar."

"What's his name?"

"Atohi. Hit means 'Woods.' Atohi's birthname was Dustu, or Sprang Frawg. Never keered fer it. He spent many a year explorin' and a-huntin' the woods to earn the nickname, Atohi. And now that's all he'll answer to."

"Tell me more about what's ahead for us. The young'uns are asking me all the time if we are going to become Indians! Or build another farm. I've run out of answers."

"Yer gonna find friends amongst 'em. They's been times they was friends with England, and sometimes enemies. Thangs are tolerable right now. But they'll take to you'uns. Robert probably tolt ye a lot about..." Moses looked shocked at his callousness. "...I mean, well..."

"Go on, Moses. Hit's alright."

"Well, you know their respect for Robert, and his father. They's a passel of colonists made friends with 'em. Lots lives thar. Matter of fact, hit commenced long 'bout 1735, I recollect, when the German, Gottlieb Priber, helped lots of colonists run off to the Cherokee—Anglish, Welsh, Germans, runaway slaves—to 'scape the British troubles. Ever since then, they's been gen'lee kind to folks on the run, and lots of 'em have set up a new life, for over a generation now."

"But a lot of them were outlaws and such, weren't they?"

"They's some what is, I reckon, and most what hain't. But we got many more outlaws a-runnin' thangs back home—I mean, back East—now, hain't we?"

"I reckon ye have to make do wherever ye are. I just pray we find good circumstances for raising my young'uns."

"I'm aimin' to fix ye up with some land use. I spec'late even more folks will be a-movin' that-away than ye even see now. Long as we keep on good terms with the Cherokee, we—that is, *you*—at least have a chance at survival. And who knows, maybe when thangs settles down, you'uns can come back to Orange County agin! Why, I'd wager on it!"

"Foreswear not the morrow."

"Eh?"

"The Lord said that. But also to pray and believe."

Moses nodded, and went off to clean the rabbits. He then went in search of edible herbs, greens, and roots to augment supper. The rabbits were soon stewing in a pot of creek water over an open fire, along with the vegetation Moses had gathered. As the sun went down, several camp fires could be seen scattered through the woods. There was a somber stillness pervading the atmosphere. Mary broke the silence by singing a hymn, soft and low, while the children one by one moved closer to her.

TURNER

As the fire died down, Mary announced, "Time for family prayer. Whose day is it?"

"Mine," answered Tipton. He began to run through the routine thanks and requests, the highlight coming in his candor as he said, "And please bless the folks back home to be happy and free, and bless the new people who are going to be helping us start over."

Mary could only stare into the remains of the fire as she quietly contemplated the youthfulness, yet the maturity, of Tipton's heartfelt prayer. A gentle pride and air of renewed confidence spread over her face. After several moments she asked, "What do you young'uns want to sing afore we go to bed?" Another soft hymn was rendered into the darkening night, bringing a sense of light as the actual fire light ebbed. Again, they all meditated in silence as the youngest began to fall asleep on Mary's lap and against her shoulders.

"The young'uns are all a-noddin' off, Mary," Moses observed.

"Better bed them down while there's still a little fire light to see by," Mary answered. She took blankets from the wagon and pitched pallets down for the older ones, and made a little bed in the wagon for Mary Ann, Joseph, and Jarred. Moses helped pick them all up and put them to bed. This got to be the routine every night on the trail.

"I sure appreciate you're helping us, Moses. And Becky, for letting you go with us," Mary said quietly.

"You'uns are worth it!" Moses replied with a wink, sauntering off to his own bedroll, holding one hand on his lower back as he attempted to straighten up.

Sunrise came as most any June day in North Carolina: beautifully backlighting through the majestic trees, awakening the songbirds, and giving a warming sense that a whole new world was being born for the good use of mankind. Mary was opening a wooden box and preparing to slice off some salt-cured ham for breakfast, when Moses came walking up from the stream.

"Save that fer the noon meal, Mary!" he cheerfully proclaimed, holding high a big mess of trout freshly caught,

BLOOD AT ALAMANCE!

already cleaned and ready for cooking. "We can have these now. The cured ham will keep. These won't."

Mary stepped down from the wagon and exclaimed with a smile, "Well, thank'ee kindly, Moses! Not sure the young'uns have ever thought about fish for breakfast. But I am sure they will be glad to have it!"

Moses handed the trout over to Mary, and set about starting a morning fire. Mary greased a big skillet with lard, sprinkled the fish in cornmeal, and soon had them frying on the fire. The aroma of food cooking began to awaken the children. One by one they came, rubbing their eyes, to give their mother a good morning hug. Moses smiled and patted juvenile heads as they filed past. Little Mary Ann asked, "Moses, why do ye have a hole in the front of ye hat?"

He poked his finger in the hole, flipped his hat off his head with it, and whirled it into a spin. "So's I kin hurry and greet folks with the fastest tippin' hat they ever saw!" he explained. His mouth fell open in mock awe. They all had a laugh, and the pleasant mood gave hint that this could be an agreeable day.

As Moses' wagon rumbled on up the trail, Mary sat in the back holding Mary Ann while Joseph and Jarred sat on the seat. Christian, Tipton, and Solomon chose to walk ahead of the wagon, playing scout and exploring the route through the heavy forest—the shadowy path that led to their vague future. Tipton noticed a crabapple tree, bearing newly forming little fruit. "Here, let's give some to the little'uns!" he said with a grin, plucking the hard green fruit which, even when ripe, is bitterly sour.

The three carried some back to their younger brothers, as Tipton gleefully announced, "Look'ee what we found ye! Apples!" They handed the boys a handful apiece.

The little boys gladly bit into them, only to be repulsed by the taste. "They're sour!" Jarred cried, and threw his apples at the older boys, now trailing behind the wagon.

"Mine, too! You meanies!" cried Joseph, likewise tossing his back at the perpetrators.

The older boys laughed. Even Christian managed a slight grin in the momentary distraction from his state of gloom. Tipton declared, "So, hit's war! I'll show you'uns how it's done!" He broke off a thin tree branch, pulled out his pocket knife, and quickly cut off its branching foliage. He then whittled a sharp tip on it, stuck it into one of the crabapples, and whipped it forward, causing it to sling at a blurring velocity. Jarred was struck on the head.

"Crabapple war!" cried Solomon.

Tipton fired off another and hit Joseph. The third one narrowly missed Mary's head and struck the horse, startling it into a quick jerk forward as it began to run wildly. It required all of Moses' skills as a wagoner to bring the beast under control. The pranksters stood with mouths agape, as the wagon disappeared over a hill. They walked slowly for several minutes, hiding from view. When Moses got down to check and adjust the harness, the horse almost bolted again, but he brought him under control.

Mary called out, "You boys, come on and catch up with us."

"Hit was Tipton what done it, Maw!" Joseph whined, still rubbing his head.

Now the horse whinnied madly, rearing and fighting to run loose. "I couldn't have scared it that much!" Tipton said, marveling. Moses grabbed the reins at the bit and hung on with all his weight. Then high up on an embankment he saw the new source of the horse's acute fright: a large mountain lion, called a *painter* by local folk, standing atop a rock outcropping growling and shaking its head as a white froth slung from its mouth.

"A mad painter!" Moses cried. "Hold the reins, Mary, in case I lose my grip!" He pulled his pistol from his belt and held the horse with his left hand while leaning across its back with his right arm. He took aim and dispatched a well-placed round into the raving beast, which tumbled down the embankment to the side of the road. The horse tried to bolt again, dragging Moses several feet until giving up the effort. Once the cat was behind and out of sight, the horse calmed considerably.

The straggling boys came running up to see what the excitement was, then slowed up as they approached the scene. They walked gingerly past the dead cat, then

BLOOD AT ALAMANCE!

caught up with the wagon, sensing their mother was no longer concerned with their disruptive antics.

"Good thing ye seen him, Moses," Tipton observed.

"*Saw* him, son," Mary corrected.

"I'd not of seen it, ordinarily. It bein' mad an 'all, it had no idee it was 'sposin' itself. Glad we seen hit 'fore hit seen us."

"*Saw*, Moses," Tipton interjected.

"Shish!" Mary whispered at Tipton. "Well, Moses, I reckon that's one more thing we have to worry about, out here, is—*painters*."

"I'd druther of seen a mad'un come out in the open, than not seen the one that come a-creepin' up on me unawares, n' tore me up!" Moses rejoined, shaking his head.

"Well, let's get on out of here, Moses! If hit's got disease!" little Mary Ann asserted.

"We can't go on just yet, right, Moses?" Mary asked.

"That's right, Mary," Moses confirmed. "Not 'til we burn the thang up. Ye see, young'uns, hit'll git ate by other critters, and then they'll catch the sickness, and hit'll spread ever-whurs!"

The big boys gathered wood for Moses, who lit a fire off the way. Using large sticks they pushed and nudged it into the fire, and piled on more wood. They kept the blaze going for a good hour, then let it die down. "Fetch my shovel out'n the wagon, Tipton," Moses directed. "Gotta kivver up this hyar far, so hit won't git out. No water hereabouts, so gotta kivver the thang up good."

Back in the wagon, Moses continued, "The Cherokee'll see the smoke, fer certain. I spec'late they'll keep a keerful eye on us all along the trail. But they know me. I'm welcome hyar." Several minutes passed when Moses spoke again. "Hit'd be a good thang fer me to sang the Cherokee morning song. They'd like that, and they'll know we're…"

"What Cherokees, Moses?" Tipton interrupted. "I don't see ary Indians!"

"Oh, they's been a-watchin' us all along." The children all cringed. "But don't ye worry. They're jes' fascinated with you'uns, is all. Here now, they'll like to hyar me a-sangin' this." Moses pulled in a good reserve of air to fill his lungs, and rang out the song like the long, steady lowing of a cow. "Wen-dey-ya-ho, wen-dey-ya-ho. Wen-de-ya, wen-dey-ya, ho-ho-ho-ho, hey-ya-ho, hey-ya-ho, ya-ya-ya!"

"What does it mean?" Mary asked.

"Well, basically, hit means 'God, I offer this day to You, for Your use'."

Having sanctified the morning and set all at peace, they rolled onward. The bigger boys were restricted to riding in the wagon for the time being. The adventures of the morning devolved into just another day, the routine of wilderness travel now proving mostly a steady, uneventful passage of time, despite occasional native eyes secretly observing their progress. Over the next hour the forest grew rather quiet, until the monotony was broken by the singing of a pair of mocking birds.

"Hark'ee! Jes' lissen to the mockin' birds!" Moses chimed in with a grin. "Hain't they purdee?"

"Oh, yes, they sure are," Mary replied. "Songs from the skies. Always good company."

"Paw-Paw loved mocking birds," little Mary Ann added. Without a second thought, her cheery face lapsed into one of dismay, then tearful sorrow. Practically on cue the eyes of the entire party began to pool up with tears. The children all began to silently and privately sob, but in deep communal earnest, as the bitter shock of sorrow shot through their hearts like a quiet lightning. Mary wiped at her eyes. Moses hid his eyes by looking off to the side, stoically tightening his face and shaking the feeling off, at least on the surface.

Mary said in a low moan, "I was sure I'd shed all the tears I'd ever have in a lifetime. Now I wish I had more." Silence again fell over the party. After a few minutes of wordless common expression of heartache, Mary added, "Hit's fine to remember ye Paw with deep feelings. A very fine thing." After more reflection she adjoined, "Just remember our morning prayer today. We started out calling for safety and peace. Part of that peace is letting the Lord take charge of our spirit."

BLOOD AT ALAMANCE!

"That's what Paw would tell us, isn't it, Maw?" Christian interjected with sudden surprise. "I mean, he was strong wasn't he. And he trusted in the Lord." It was Christian's moment of breakthrough—his total epiphany through the barriers of heart, mind, and soul which had so beset him.

"Why, Christian! That is the best thing anybody could say. And all true!" Mary replied, looking back at him with the broadest smile she had expressed in many days. Christian reciprocated with a beaming smile so typical of his true self, as if a rebirth had formed within his soul. Like a beam of light from Heaven, an illuminating bridge was suddenly constructing between Christian and the humanity he so mourned for. Mary reached her arm out to him and took him by the hand, pulling him up to the wagon seat where he nudged in between her and Moses. They rode along smiling for several minutes, when Mary called out for song suggestions. Once the children were singing together, smiles beamed through their teary faces, and soon merriment reigned over misery.

By late afternoon Moses reined up at a narrow pass flanked by two large outcroppings of rock. He made a whistling sound like a bird, and waited. Within two minutes two Cherokee men appeared. Moses climbed down and spoke with them, and gave them each a blanket, axe, and a horn of gunpowder in trade for transitory land usage. The men nodded stoically and motioned for Moses to lead the Messer party onward into Cherokee lands. With that passage, the Messer history ended for a time. No further word was ever heard of them eastward.

They rode along for another hour until the trail was too narrow for the wagon. "What do we do now, Moses?" Mary asked.

"Jes' ye come and see!" he answered. Helping her down from the seat, he bade her follow him to a low thicket. "Just look'ee over yanner!"

Cherokee villagers were cooking their evening meal over fires. Moses recited his bird whistle again, and they looked quickly toward him. Then smiling, many of them stood and extended their arms in a gesture of welcome.

TURNER

Moses whispered, "Hate to say so, Mary, but hit'd be a good thang to let ye hair down, like they wears theirs hyar. Ye'd look more natcherul amongst 'em."

"You young'uns, come here!" Mary called, as she unpinned her long brown hair and let it fall, shaking her head about. The Cherokee were motioning for them to enter their village. Slowly Mary followed Moses, as the children followed her. Seeing so many friendly faces, she could not resist returning the gesture as a meek but warm smile erupted through her drawn and weary countenance like a self-sculpting visage.

"And look'ee over yanner," Moses said, pointing across a narrow river. "And up yan way!" He nodded toward the low ridges overlooking the green valley. "See them white folks? They's folks just like you'uns. Regulators, many of 'em. Ye'll find a new life hyar, Mary. New folks, for makin' new friends and families." Mary observed in silence as he went on. "Now and then thar'll be a runaway slave amongst the tribe, but they keep 'em well hid from bounty hunters."

Moses stretched out his arm toward Mary and the children, and introduced them to the village with one word: "Messer!" The gathering of hosts recited the word deliciously, "MAY-sah! MAY-sah!" In unison they began to nod acceptance, as reverence for the Messer name reflected in the depth of their eyes. Many of the whites came down from the ridges and waded the stream, to join the welcoming rites. Young braves ran up and stood sharing curious stares with the new boys in their village. Young girls came and marveled over pretty little Mary Ann, running their hands through her glossy, curly hair. She folded her hands and sat on a boulder, smiling like a proud little princess from the attention and instant celebrity.

Some of the women introduced themselves to Mary. One smiled and pointed at herself, saying, "Immookalee!"

Moses explained, "You just met Water Fall!"

Mary returned the smile and attempted to repeat the name, "Imma—Immaka..."

The group laughed as the woman repeated, "Immookalee!"

BLOOD AT ALAMANCE!

Others introduced themselves as "Anagaluskee," and "Hiawassee."

"And they are Flowery Branch and Meadow," Moses clarified. Pointing at Mary and then to the women, Moses said, "Galiheli tsidenalv!" He explained to Mary, "I jes' said 'happy to meet ye!'" Mary nodded politely.

As tribesmen approached Moses with hearty greetings, he turned and said, "And hyar's a chief, Yonaguska, and Kanagagota—Standing Turkey…" The boys giggled, but quickly ceased when Moses gave a stern shake of the head. "…and this hyar's my old friend, Mo-he, The Elk."

In no time at all Mary was sitting with women, watching them make baskets and jugs, while Mary Ann played with the village girls and their dolls made of buckskin, feeling quite at home with their surprisingly common interests. The boys were running about the woods playing adventurous games with their new native friends, as naturally as boys will do.

They had found a home.

The sun which had gone down on an exhausting day arose with the promise of new beginnings. The Messers did not notice as Moses turned about with a satisfied grin, and stepped lively toward his wagon from which he began to unload goods and food for them. Within moments he was wheeling away. He stopped for one last look over his shoulder and said to himself with a nod, "Yep, a new home, and a new history!"

Facing eastward, he slapped reins and drifted back toward the past. He pondered an acorn as it fell in the trail, and how, unless unnaturally disturbed, it could flourish into a mighty oak. Like the handful of human acorns he had delivered to safe and fertile soil, the future of freedom lay behind him.

EPILOGUE

Mary Messer: After years of hardship for Mary and her children, their descendants went on to thrive in western North Carolina and eastern Tennessee. A large Messer Family Association exists today to research and preserve their genealogy, and to pay tribute to the contributions to American liberty made by this family.

Christian Messer: Christian served throughout the entire seven years of the Revolutionary War, enlisted as a private and discharged a captain.

James Few: His gravesite is unknown. After the Battle of Alamance his family fled to Georgia, where his brothers Benjamin and William became prominent Revolutionary officers. William went on to become a Congressman and Senator, and a signer of the Constitution.

Herman Husband: Herman never even knew the Battle of Alamance was taking place, though he was blamed for it. He reached his native Pennsylvania where he became a leader in the Revolution, and in state government. He spent his life championing movements for safeguarding liberty and the fair treatment of citizens. Some sources refer to him as Harmon Husbands.

William Tryon: Eleven days after the last hangings at Hillsborough, Tryon was at sea, bound from New Bern to New York to accept his assignment from King George III to serve as Governor there. He unsuccessfully fought against American forces in the Revolutionary War, earning much hatred by burning the crops and farms of innocent civilians in Connecticut in an attempt to draw Gen. Washington away from the Hudson Valley. Both sides despised him for

BLOOD AT ALAMANCE!

"waging war on women and children." He died in London in 1788, never facing trial for the many atrocities he committed against the Carolinians and New Englanders entrusted to his care.

Edmund Fanning: Fanning followed Tryon to New York as his personal secretary. He raised a regiment of Loyalists in the war. He fled with them to Nova Scotia in 1783, where he became Lt. Governor. In 1786 he was appointed Governor of the Province of St. John's Island (now Prince Edward Island). Promoted to General in 1808, he later retired in London where he died in 1818. He finally married at 46; no one knows the ultimate fate of the fiancée he stole from James Few. He was never tried for his atrocities against fellow American colonials.

King George III: The King eventually showed forth a measure of pity on a few of the North Carolinians, no doubt following stories of Tryon's atrocities. He granted that Jemimah Merrill would retain ownership of her husband Benjamin's plantation, and freed six condemned Regulators whom Tryon left languishing in jail after his departure to New York: Forrester Mercer, James Stewart, James Emerson, Herman Cox, William Brown, and James Copeland.

Alamance County, NC: In 1849, the western half of Orange County was renamed Alamance County.

Gov. Josiah Martin: He replaced Tryon as Governor of North Carolina on August 11, 1771. He initially shared the British bias against the backcountry Carolinians until he toured the area. He then wrote his superiors that the Regulators "had been provoked by insolence and cruelty... by mercenary tricking attorneys, clerks, and officers... whose treachery drove them to acts of desperation in order to survive... and rather than being objects of hatred, they deserve the government's pity."

TURNER

Tryon's Palace: Four years after the Battle of Alamance, Gov. Martin fled the palace at the beginning of the American Revolution. The North Carolinians seized it and proclaimed it their new state capitol building.

Tryon County: In 1768 Governor-General Tryon persuaded the Colonial Assembly to create a new county and name it after him, in southwestern North Carolina. It never had a chance to prosper or develop, let alone carry on his vile name. In 1779 the State of North Carolina dissolved it, creating in its stead Lincoln and Rutherford Counties.

American Revolution: Most scholars call Alamance the first battle of the American Revolution, though it took place four years before Concord and Lexington. Some claim it was not, saying the fight was against a Royal governor and not the King directly; but it actually was caused by the same kinds of oppression as took place in New England. Moreover, the news of what happened at Alamance was excitedly discussed all over the American Colonies: That decent folk had stood up against corruption for the cause of liberty, which gave hope and impetus to all American Patriots who fought for our freedom. The fire of freedom sparked in Alamance!

BLOOD AT ALAMANCE!

HISTORICAL MARKER IN HILLSBOROUGH, NC

ഌൣ

www.ingramcontent.com/pod-product-compliance
Lightning Source LLC
Chambersburg PA
CBHW051757040426
42446CB00007B/405